SOUTHEND
Memories

DEE GORDON

SUTTON PUBLISHING

First published in 2006 by
Sutton Publishing Limited · Phoenix Mill
Thrupp · Stroud · Gloucestershire · GL5 2BU

Dee Gordon has asserted the moral right
to be identified as the author of this work.

British Library Cataloguing in Publication Data
A catalogue record for this book is available from the British Library

ISBN 0-7509-4369-6

Typeset in 11/12pt Ehrhardt.
Typesetting and origination by
Sutton Publishing Limited.
Printed and bound in England by
J.H. Haynes & Co. Ltd, Sparkford.

CONTENTS

PREFACE

Like so many east Londoners, I was a frequent day tripper to Southend-on-Sea – sometimes by train, sometimes by charabanc – in the 1950s, which many of the people in this book will regard as the heyday of its popularity. Even the sun seemed to shine day after day, and there was a naivety, an innocence about the place and its people, residents and visitors alike; everyone revelled in the relief of a postwar world. From the autobiographical reminiscences of Charlie Chaplin through to Charlie Richardson (a contemporary of the Krays), the world and his wife seemed to enjoy visiting Southend.

The 1960s saw more than just the national influences of music, foreign travel, television, fashion, the motor car and the cult of the teenager; it saw the arrival of high-rise blocks completely changing the look of the town centre. The standard of living improved immeasurably during this decade, not that material deprivation marred youthful pleasures – as you will see from the reminiscences that follow.

Mary Hopkin's 1968 song said it all: 'Those Were The Days'.

Dee Gordon

ACKNOWLEDGEMENTS

Simon Fletcher and his team at Sutton Publishing have made this book a pleasure to write, but lots of people have helped it to fruition. Principally, I owe a vote of thanks to those interviewees included in these pages, who tolerated a barrage of questions, and were all so willing and happy to share their memories, almost invariably fond ones, of a time and a place tinged with a very deep rose.

There were people who helped me source those with memories of the 1950s and 1960s, especially Donna Lowe, Pat Stone, Roger Robinson, Kim Kimber, Judith Williams, Emma Bearman and Alison Halton, as well as staff at the Southend Library and Southend Museum who helped me check some locations and some occasionally dubious facts; and people who provided photographs, particularly Gary Nicholls and John Atkins, some of which I was unable to use for reasons of space, principally those from David Goody, Dorothy West and Bob Essery.

Thanks also to the staff and residents of Beaufort Lodge, St Vincents Road, Westcliff, whose memories of the era and the town were so diverse.

HARRY DAY

Southend's Frank Sinatra?

Although Harry is not strictly a Southender, as he was born in Kent at the end of the First World War, he has been in the area since 1945 and has become a well-known character in the town. As a musician and singer, he had moved to London to find band work. A couple of pals he came across at the Locarno in Tottenham Court Road told him about a vacancy for a drummer with Stan Pearse at a phenomenal (if his memory serves him correctly) £9 per week. He joined the band the next day and was subsequently offered a job in Southend at Mecca's Olympia Ballroom at the bottom of Pier Hill, a venue reachable only by escalator. This is where he met his wife, Rose, an usherette, and they married at St John's Church at the end of the 1940s, with Mecca providing a plush reception.

Harry (on the drums) with Stan Pearse (piano) and Guy Snowden (saxophone) at the Olympia Ballroom, Pier Hill, c. 1953. (Day collection: original photo Star Photography, Leigh)

Harry Day and baby Sue (aged about 3 months) in the back garden of their Fairfax Drive home, early 1950s. (Day collection)

Harry and Rose started married life with her mum and brothers in St Leonard's Road, Southend, with a sheet of hardboard on one of the beds as a table. Professionally, he moved on to the Kursaal with Howard Baker's twenty-one piece band, and performed in the pubs at lunchtime with Sid Uren for extra money. It was Sid who offered the couple a share of his home in Fairfax Drive, enabling them to live downstairs while Sid and his family lived upstairs. This is where they have lived ever since, although now they have the whole house! Their three daughters were born in the 1950s in Rochford Hospital.

Although Harry had a heart attack in 1953 just after getting a standing ovation for his solo demonstration of 'Drumming Man', he is convinced this was because he was burning the candle at both ends rather than as a result of his energetic performance. While in hospital, another local musician, Harry Brooker (father of Gary of Procul Harum fame), visited him and offered him a job in a six-piece band, Felix Mendelssohn and his Hawaiian Serenaders.

He worked with them for three years at the Palace Hotel. In the 1950s this venue featured plush red carpets, even on the pavements outside, and gold-braided commissionaires escorting ladies in from their 'carriages'. Its Blue Room Restaurant was one of the more superior in the town at the time. In 1952, Laurel and Hardy appeared at the Palace, and Harry found Stan Laurel particularly friendly. In fact, as one of Harry's daughters had been born at the same juncture, Stan accompanied Harry home to 'wet the baby's head' with whisky, much to the amazement of Rose.

While with the Hawaiian Serenaders, Harry wore the appropriate dress code – black baggy trousers, flowery shirts and leis around the neck. He worked six days a week (including Sunday lunchtime, but not Sunday evenings – and no dance music was allowed on Sundays), singing and drumming, but also took on extra work in the building trade.

By the late 1950s, Harry was back with Howard Baker and his Broadcasting Band, touring as far afield as Northampton at a time before motorways. Their sessions could finish at one o'clock in the morning, leaving Harry with very little spare time. In the meantime, Rose was taking the children to the boating lake that was then alongside the Pier, and to Never Never Land, always a girly favourite with its turreted castles. When the girls were very small, the prime baby-goods supplier in the town was Liddiard's in Victoria Avenue (now Kindercare), and Harry persuaded Ray Liddiard over a drink in the Spread Eagle to provide them with a Silver Cross pram for the twins they thought they were expecting. It transpired that twins didn't materialise until the second pregnancy, so they did get the Silver Cross eventually. The girls went to Macdonalds Junior School, then Dowsett School.

Holidays were brief and at short notice, but they did manage to take advantage of £2 return day trips to Ostend from Southend airport, leaving at eight in the morning and back at six in the evening. This was a one-hour journey on a Viscount eighty-seater, and the children travelled free of charge.

Harry's memories of the music scene in Southend are far-ranging. He recalls the Glide-a-drome by the seafront gasworks, which featured roller skating alongside a big band. There was a ballroom at the beginning of the Pier, and a sun deck at the end that also featured a band under cover. Apart from the Kursaal and Olympia ballrooms, every pub along the Esplanade to the Halfway House had a live band, with punters ready and willing to put money in the band's post-performance collecting box. Jukeboxes in pubs later killed off the live bands.

The seafront in the 1950s was awash with day trippers, with trains into London running every ten minutes. There was hardly any traffic along the beachside roads apart from coaches and buses. Mondays were traditionally ladies' days, when the young and old arrived on coaches laden with beer, and were not averse to flashing red, white and blue knickers – just for fun. It seems that this kind of bawdy revelry was common after the war, when ladies from London arrived, allegedly to avoid paying their rent, but it was less common by the 1950s. The Kursaal's funfair and its gardens were a big attraction, with an entrance fee of around 3*d*, and Harry has fond memories of the caterpillar and the water chute and particularly of the wind tunnel (controlled by Kursaal staff, which blew the girls' skirts up. It seems that Tornado Smith from the Kursaal's Wall of Death liked a drink at the Victoria Hotel (then at Victoria Circus) before his performances. Harry often picked him up there and took him to the Kursaal.

The 1960s saw Harry back with the Sid Uren Trio, performing straight dance music. One of their first jobs was at the restaurant then in Southend airport, which it seems was quite something, with first-class cuisine at around £3–4 a head. They were the resident band there for two years, and it was a very busy period for Harry, who was expanding his building business during the day. When the band moved on to the Commodore (brand new and elite) at Basildon, customers from the airport followed them.

It was important that Harry kept up with changes in the music world, and in drumming in particular, and Ringo Starr had quite an influence on him and his peers because of the new beat patterns he introduced. The Beatles also brought the guitar into the limelight, and were instrumental – literally – in bringing an end to Sunday restrictions on music.

The early 1960s saw the formation of the Harry Day Combo, which lasted until the 1980s. They were resident for a number of years at the Queen's Hotel, then in Hamlet Court Road, Westcliff, a resplendent pub and hotel, but played other venues such as the Dorchester in Park Lane. At the Queen's Hotel, famous names appeared before they were famous – Bob Monkhouse, Leo Sayer, Genesis, ELO and Suzi Quatro, who appeared at the age of 17 for just £5 expenses. Lots of Masonic lodges had their dos here, and Harry, as musical director, had the freedom to choose the music, suiting it to the patrons.

During this period at the Queen's, he organised Sunday mornings for the children known as 'Grown Ups Mind Your Own Business'. This brought a couple of hundred children in, and their parents would use the time in the hotel's bars. Stars from the Cliffs Pavilion visited on Sundays and signed autographs for the children – people such as Ann Shelton and Edmund Hockridge. When West Ham were playing at Southend, all the team came along with footballs for their young fans. A feature of these Sunday mornings was an ongoing talent competition, with the final judged by one of the visiting stars. Prize money amounted to about £60. Music was obviously an important part of Sunday's entertainment, and there were treats on special days. For example, on Mother's Day 'Uncle Harry' presented the youngsters with violets, which they could give to their mums on stage. The regulars among the children even had their own committee to keep an eye out for bad behaviour and nip it in the bud.

Harry (on the left) and the Queen's Hotel staff with their carnival float, late 1960s. (Day collection)

*Harry with John Inman (*Are You Being Served?*) on Southend Pier at the 50th anniversary of Laurel and Hardy's visit to Southend, 2002.* (Day collection)

At carnival time, the Queen's had its own float, and the Harry Day Combo was featured. One float was set up as a garden with umbrellas, paid for by Fosters Lager, but when it was finished it was too big to get out of the Queen's gates, so the sides had to be removed and replaced. Although this was a four-and-a-half-hour drive, these carnival processions are remembered with great affection.

Harry has had several opportunities over the years to reminisce about this period in the local press, and even with Chris Tarrant on television.

HARRY WEST

Dib Dob and Bob a Job

arry (born in Summercourt Road, Westcliff, in 1920) started his Scouting life before the Second World War, and came out of it wanting to form his own group, to 'do something' for the boys. Another inspiration was an uncle who was a Scout leader.

By trade, he became a butcher, and he married in 1941. In the 1950s his wife, Gladys, was beginning to epitomise the idea of a Scout widow, although she had her own interests; for instance, she sang in the Salvation Army choir until the children came along. The Salvation Army was also important to Harry. He played the tuba, having been taught by the junior band leader at Southend Citadel. On the evenings Harry was out either Gladys or her mother looked after the children at the family home in Kensington Road, Southend. This was to be their home for over fifty-seven years, and was rented out by the landlord living next door, who

Harry West is the one with the largest tuba! The Salvation Army Essex International Jamboree at Belchamps, Hockley, 1952. (West collection: original photo Rimmer, Leigh)

did not want to sell because, if he did, he would have no control over his neighbours.

By 1950, Harry was the district Scout leader, the local association having grown so much that it had been divided into districts. This meant he was out visiting other troops in the area, such as Rochford, Prittlewell or Southchurch. Three years later, after the Scouts had changed from King Scouts to Queen Scouts, he became East district commissioner (for Southend and Prittlewell Scouts). For this role he had undertaken a course in Chingford, and an assessment by the district commissioner, at the end of which he had achieved the accolade of Wood Badge. This uniform he wore with pride for over thirty years.

When he handed over the Scout leadership for Southend, the troop had forty Cubs and twenty Scouts, and the boys saw it as somewhere to achieve, and the badges as something to strive for. Promotion meant that he was now authorised to present warrants to leaders, and ensure there were enough of them, and that everyone obeyed the Scouting rules. In the 1950s, there were possibly more female Cub Scout leaders than male, and they were invariably middle-aged or older. Leaders, male or female, were known then, as now, as Akela, and the Scoutmaster was invariably known as Skip.

In 1952, the first Essex International Jamboree was held at Belchamps camp in Hawkwell. This attracted Scouts from Sweden, Denmark and Holland, and from countries as far away as Korea. The Renewal of Promise Parades were something of a public relations exercise in the 1950s and 1960s. The parades, of some 1,500 Scouts, moved from St John's Road in Westcliff, past the war memorial and the bandstand to the Odeon in Southend High Street. There the flags of all the Scouting groups would be on the stage. Two Scout bands were a part of these parades, boosted by the Southend Citadel Salvation Army band, which provided the music for the service.

Even Harry's annual holidays were dictated by the timing of Scout camp trips. His wife and children (three by now, one having died at a very young age) would visit the camp on Parents' Day, but their holiday was more often a day trip to Canvey Island on the bus. Scouting was also Harry's social life, what with going to band practice on Thursdays, visiting camps on Saturdays, arranging and attending meetings, organising carol services at Christmas, and keeping up to date with Scouting changes.

Harry on a Scouting course in 1953. (West collection)

The Second Southend Scout troop outside the Salvation Army hall, Clarence Street, preparing for a camping trip in the 1950s. (West collection)

To get around from one troop to another, he relied mainly on his bicycle, but occasionally borrowed the butcher's van, having passed his driving test in 1948. (He did not get his first car until 1959.) As a butcher Harry had worked for Garons in Southend High Street, the 'Butchers under the Bridge'. But in the 1950s and for most of the 1960s he worked, less conveniently, in Romford.

He had to find the money for two uniforms – the Scouts and the Salvation Army. On Sundays he played with the Salvation Army band at their open-air services morning and evening, and marched with them before and after the services. The band was about forty-strong at one point. On his afternoon off, Harry and his family enjoyed visiting Joe Lyons in Southend High Street. They treated themselves to a plate of chips each, and walked back home down Pier Hill. Southchurch Park was another favourite family venue. When the children were

Harry receiving the new district union flag from the minister of Wesley Church, Leigh-on-Sea,
c. *1954.* (West collection)

older, Gladys worked for a while as a school dinner lady at Bournemouth Park School.

Harry can recall just one Scout show in the 1950s, held at the Kursaal as part of a Scouting bonanza, which was advertised on one of Southend's carnival floats, which sported the flags of all the countries that were involved. In the 1960s, however, the Scouts' shows became a regular feature at the Palace Theatre, London Road, Westcliff. Senior Scouts such as Harry took turns to look after visiting dignitaries such as the Southend mayor, taking them backstage to meet the cast.

By this time Harry's own son, Derek, had become a Cub, but he was less enthusiastic about the Scouts, who all seemed so much bigger than him! Derek was keener on sport, especially football, and became captain of his school football team (Southchurch Hall School), and head boy by the end of the 1960s. He also played baritone brass in the Salvation Army's junior band for a while, and all the children attended Sunday school at the Southend Citadel while Harry was at the open-air services.

There was a national Scouting review in 1966, when the uniform changed from hats to berets and from shorts to trousers, with some changes to the badge system. This was mainly to bring the fraternity up to date, and to a lesser extent because boys were growing more aware of, and interested in, what they wore. Part of Harry's role was to implement these changes.

Harry, who is still known as Skip to generations of Scouts, has finally retired and remains a resident of Southend.

GLADYS MUDE MBE

Music, Music, Music

Since the early 1920s Gladys has always lived in Southend, although she has seen many changes over the years. Her family moved to the house where she now lives shortly after the Second World War. Her mother encouraged her to take an interest in music, especially singing and the piano, which she began to learn at the age of 6. Although Mum occasionally earned a few pence an hour for babysitting or did a bit of cleaning, she appears to have given up her job as a professional cook when Gladys came along. Dad provided the family income as a decorator, but his wages suffered if it rained.

For Gladys, therefore, her dream of being a teacher did not seem possible, given that she felt the need to contribute to the household's finances. She was working at E.K. Cole in 1948 when, as a result of teacher shortages, an emergency training scheme was initiated. Following an interview at Chelmsford, Gladys was offered a place on a one-year crash course at Bedford. This was far more affordable, and the training was of a good standard, involving three months of primary school practice, with a choice of specialisations. Gladys chose singing and the violin. She then had two years' probationary teaching at West Leigh Schools.

At this time, the early 1950s, Southend had a lot of choirs – male, ladies', mixed, children's and choral societies. Gladys's own singing teacher Madame Parry (Madame apparently indicated that she was married but was used with the teacher's maiden name for professional reasons) won a first prize with the Freda Parry's Ladies' Choir at the Festival of Britain, which took place on London's South Bank in 1951. The prize, a silver rose bowl, is on display at Porter's, the mayor's official residence on the corner of Grange Gardens, Southend. Madame Parry lived in Westbourne Grove for many years, and had a small chain of music academies, one apparently in Hamlet Court Road. When conducting the Junior Co-op Choir (a choir of youngsters whose parents were members of the Co-operative Society, now known as the Southend Young Singers) Madame Parry had a heart attack, resulting in her death in 1971.

As for Gladys, she was granted a music scholarship to the Guildhall in London, but she could not be spared from West Leigh. Later, when she could be spared for a one-year part-time course, it turned out to be unpaid, so Gladys had to do temporary secretarial work in London to be able to take advantage of the opportunity. But she qualified and returned to West Leigh Schools, later transferring to Bournemouth Park Girls' School until the end of the 1950s.

Gladys Mude is standing on the left of Revd Mr Erskine from St Mary's in Hobbs Ward, Southend Hospital, following a Sunday morning service in the early 1960s. (Mude collection)

At this time she learned to drive, having used a bicycle to get around up to now. The last words from her instructor before she passed her test were: 'Please don't swear at the pedestrians.' It seems she was very ashamed of her first car, which seemed to be of mismatched colours inside and out, with a primitive, indescribable, braking system.

In the meantime brother Norman, a rep, who had been in the Fleet Air Arm during the war, married the Wren he had met all those years before. They had a flat in Southview Drive, Westcliff, then a bungalow in Rochford, but after the children came along (a boy and a girl) Norman's employers moved to Liverpool, and the family left the area.

Back in Southend, Gladys was actively involved with the Southend Competitive Music Festival, which took place every November at different venues in the town, and the Leigh Festival, which took place in spring at the Leigh Community Centre. These established events were for adults and children alike, who would compete for different classes in piano, elocution, strings, mime and choirs, with the standard at gold-medal class being on a par with professional musicians. Gladys was personally successful in the singing classes – soprano, mezzo, contralto – and in piano. On Saturday evenings, finals night, you had to get there at teatime to get a seat, it seems, and Mum bicycled over in good time and sat through it all, enthralled. Dad was not so keen. He found it a tad repetitive, as many of the performances repeated the same pieces of music. Gladys's brother, Norman, was encouraged to learn the violin, but she does not remember it ever coming out of its case, except to hit someone on one occasion!

By now, Gladys had long been involved as a volunteer at Southend Hospital, a lifelong commitment for which she was later (much, much later) awarded an MBE. In the 1950s this saw her playing the piano and singing hymns for five separate Sunday services, in three women's and two men's wards. Each ward had its own piano, and she and the minister from St Mary's Church were accompanied by whoever was on duty at the time – the nurses, sister, deputy matron, hospital domestics – and soon hymn books were distributed to patients, and a good time was had by all. In the 1960s, the pianos gradually died a natural, tuneful, death, it not being viable to maintain them, and the accompanying minister changed too, to the St Peter's representative; however, the hymns and services carried on.

As if that was not enough, Gladys was also involved in the setting-up of a nurses' choir, which anyone could join. It was easier to coordinate practice sessions when all the nurses lived in, as they did then. There were nurses' homes at Southend and Rochford hospitals, both providing rehearsal space. The nurses' choir won the Stratford Competitive Musical Competition choral class three times in the 1960s.

Life as a teacher meant that any other spare time was often occupied with homework, after-school activities, hockey matches, choir practice and so on. Occasionally, Gladys would attend a local dance with her brother, apart from the annual hospital dances at such venues as the Kursaal in Southend, or the Arlington Rooms at Chalkwell. Dances at the latter would be rather short of men until someone hit on the idea of inviting men from the Shoebury Garrison, which seemed to solve the problem. Mum would accompany her on occasion to the Palace Theatre in London Road, Westcliff, or to a Sunday afternoon classical concert there. There were also shows-cum-concerts from the Southend Music Club at the Queen's Hotel in Hamlet Court Road.

The nurses' choir in full song at the Salvation Hall in Leigh in the 1950s, with Gladys playing piano on the left. (Mude collection)

This is the Ritz Children's Choir – from the Southend cinema – who had just won the area finals, c. 1959, and were looking forward to the finals at the Odeon, Leicester Square, to be followed by a visit to the circus. Gladys, their pianist, is on the right, with the conductor, Leslie Price, behind her, and Mr Nimse, the cinema manager, next to him. (Mude collection)

A new post of 'special responsibility' was Gladys's next professional role when she moved to Temple Sutton Primary, Eastern Avenue, Southend. She was there for seven years, although the 'special responsibility' seemed more about being able to order needlework supplies than anything else.

Finally, in 1966, she achieved deputy head status – at Hamstel primary – and settled there until her retirement sixteen years later. Here, she was responsible for discipline, for teachers who needed her help, and for the administration of punishments; but she never felt the need to use the cane. She did, however, always feel the need to be extra strict from September to Christmas so that she could relax over Christmas and help out by decorating the classrooms, allowing her warmer nature to show through.

Overall, Gladys has only fond memories of the pupils and teachers she came across in her career. There were the identical triplets who liked to confuse her – and the other teachers – by switching places. There was the disabled boy with a twisted, corseted body who could manage PE but who needed, and got, plenty of assistance from his peers in rewrapping the corset afterwards. And there was the boy who practised a wrestling hold on his friend who promptly passed out and had to be revived, giving everyone quite a scare.

Gladys remains in Southend, a busy lady, with fond memories.

RON STOKOE

Taxis, Time and Motion

Ron was just a toddler when his family moved to the area from Lambeth in south London in the 1930s. He married Iris, from Rainham, in 1951 at St Mary's, Prittlewell, and soon after moved to a rented flat in Southchurch Road. Ron remembers this as having a huge lounge and a proper bathroom, and, although not self-contained, it even had its own garden. Their furniture was mostly purchased from Norris's in Southend High Street, with a small amount paid weekly covering everything they needed for the flat.

While still in this flat, the children, Jack and Lorraine, were born at Rochford Hospital in 1953 and 1956 respectively. Ron vividly recalls snow-white nappies hanging on the washing line in spite of the absence of a washing machine, thanks to his wife's expertise with the scrubbing board. The Swan pram, with the latest anti-tipping brake, was bought at Liddiard's in Victoria Avenue, now Kindercare. The carrycot with Jack in it was perched next to the radiogram, and Ron feels this is why Jack grew up to be such a music fiend.

Traffic-free Priory Avenue, Southend, in the early 1950s, Ron Stokoe's home before marriage. (Stokoe collection)

Ron and Iris marrying at St Mary's, 1951. (Stokoe collection: original photo Star Photography, Leigh)

Iris walked everywhere with the pram, from Southchurch to central Southend and further afield, providing exercise for herself and entertainment for the children. Before the children were born Iris was a clippie on the blue trolley buses, wearing trousers and a cap as part of her uniform. It seems that the trolley-bus commuters from Leigh-on-Sea to Southend were known as 'bread-and-cheesers' because of the lunches they carried to work on a daily basis. On one occasion at Warrior Square, the ultra-lightweight Iris was hoisted up bodily when trying to stabilise the trolley bus from behind, and ended up looking at the bemused passengers from the *outside* of the upstairs rear window!

At this time, the early 1950s, Ron was a taxi-driver. He still has his Hackney Carriage Badge no. 171. Fares at the time were 1*s* 6*d* for the first mile, 1*s* for each mile thereafter, 3*d* for baggage and 6*d* extra (each) for more than two passengers. Rules and regulations for cabs and cab-drivers in those days included the necessity for running boards, and he had to get out and open the door for his customers. He ended up with three private-hire vehicles as well as his taxi, and ran the business with a partner as S & S Hire Service (Stokoe and Smith). The private-hire vehicles were based at their shop premises at Prittlewell station, and the business was busy enough to merit employing several part-time drivers.

One of Ron's taxi 'fleet', early 1950s. (Stokoe collection)

Ron himself mainly operated from the taxi rank outside Southend Central station, for which privilege he had to pay an annual fee. The hours were very long, with days starting at about 8 a.m. and often ending up at 1.30 a.m. (that is, the next morning), not ideal for a young husband with a growing family. Some days he could sit all day on the rank and not get a single fare, as happened twice in one week one winter in the 1950s, although holiday times and Christmas were usually lucrative.

He recalls a very foggy, wintry night when a passenger wanted to go to Tyrone Road in Thorpe Bay, and Ron made the decision to go along the seafront. But by the time he got to the end of Pier Hill he could not see a thing, so the passenger got out and walked in front of the cab, with Ron following him with his lights on. When they finally arrived at Tyrone Road, Ron was still paid because the passenger felt sorry for him.

One of Ron's most interesting anecdotes is of the time he picked up Laurel and Hardy from Southend Central in 1952. The manager of the Odeon in Southend High Street, where they were set to appear, reserved a car to collect them from a particular train, and Ron judged himself lucky to get the job. Oliver Hardy sat in the front, and Stan Laurel in the back in between the two wives, but the journey was very brief as they were only going as far as the Palace Hotel at the top of Pier Hill. The doorman was looking out for them, and it was the manager of the Odeon, not the stars, who paid Ron the princely sum of 7s 6d. He did get a free ticket for the show as a bonus.

During this period, Ron also took Max Miller from the Regal Theatre in Tylers Avenue to a private address in Chalkwell (apparently to a party), the fare

Ron featured in an EKCO advert in 1959 in British Plastics *magazine.* (Stokoe collection, with thanks to Ian Cosgrove, Linpac)

Bigger — than any injection moulding ever produced in Britain

Better — in appearance and finish

Quicker — produces 35 liners per hour each of 104 oz.

The completed liner showing the high gloss internal finish

This interior liner for Frigidaire's new MZ-33 household refrigerator is a single injection moulding — the largest yet produced in Britain. With a shot weight of 104 oz., these mouldings are being produced from Bextrene high impact polystyrene by Ekco Plastics Ltd. of Southend on a giant 73-ton Windsor machine

This technique for producing large articles from polystyrene in one operation means that glistening, pearlescent finishes, with high abrasion resistance, are no longer confined to relatively small components

The natural choice of material was

BEXTRENE BC.15

toughened polystyrene

Bextrene and Bextrene BC.15 (toughened) polystyrenes are unsurpassed for mouldings of any size. Write for publication number 582

BX PLASTICS LIMITED Higham Station Avenue, London E.4   LARkswood 5511
A subsidiary of The British Xylonite Company Limited

TA2244

20   British Plastics, April 1959

paid by the manager of the Regal. This was unusual, because Max Miller apparently preferred travelling everywhere in his own Rolls-Royce. As far as Ron was concerned, the comedian came across as miserable and egotistical, quite unlike his stage persona.

By 1954, more people were owning cars and the business began to suffer, so Ron changed to something more profitable, securing a job as a press operator at EKCO in Priory Crescent. The company, which made radios, televisions, radar and plastic casings, was one of Southend's biggest employers for many years. Ron was employed there until redundancy hit in the late 1970s.

His first job on the factory floor was very noisy, and he was keen to gain promotion, which meant he had to work on all sections. However, by putting in overtime and doing shifts he could double his £7 per week basic salary. The long hours were not what he had had in mind, though, now that he had two young

Roots Hall stadium in the 1950s, home of Southend United. (David Goody collection)

children, and he was pleased to be offered a 9-to-5 job in Time and Motion – except that this was less money. He negotiated a good deal for himself for an increase after a three-month trial period, and this paid off. Iris also worked at EKCO part-time for a while in the mid-1960s in the evenings. Her job was in the coil-winding department for electrical products.

Looking back on the 1950s, Ron remembers the main entertainment as being the wealth of cinemas in Southend at the time, plus Saturday morning pictures at the Odeon for the children. There were cinemas at Shoebury and Southchurch, and in Southend there was Garons, the Gaumont, the Strand, the Civic News, the Odeon (formerly Astoria), the Rivoli, the Ritz, plus the Mascot and Metropole at Westcliff, the Corona and Coliseum at Leigh, and the Kingsway at Hadleigh.

Before his children were born, Ron and Iris also went to Margate on day trips by boat from Southend Pier, and frequented dance halls at the Palace, the Kursaal and the Queen's Hotel. Ron was also a season-ticket holder for Southend United from the 1950s, and was at the memorable match when they played Manchester City in the mud and pelting rain. This was the 1956 match when the German goalkeeper, Bert Trautmann, finished the game with a suspected broken neck. The spectators knew that the goalie was in trouble because the trainer kept coming on, but not the extent of the problem.

In 1957 the growing Stokoe family moved to a council flat in Denton Avenue, Prittlewell, and when the children were at school Iris got a job as the manageress of the Leigh DIY centre in Leigh Road. Ron, too, helped out for free on Saturday mornings during their busy period, and as a result the owners of the shop became friends. They were offered a derelict flat over a second shop in Leigh rent free in lieu of salary increases for Iris, and they took up the offer in 1967. Ron did it up to make it habitable, and increased the value for its owner, while they saved for a mortgage, which finally meant they were able to own their own home in Westcliff in 1971. And Ron has been there ever since.

COUNCILLOR RAY DAVY

The Beautiful Game

Councillor Davy moved to Southend from east London in 1944, when the resort was a 'ghost town' and you had to have permission (and a job) to move to the town. He lived in Kensington Road as a child with his mum, dad and two sisters, and remembers life being very different after the war – bananas and oranges were new and exciting, with Christmas celebrated in a big way. His dad was a driver for Jacobs, the British Rail carriers, distributing parcels around Southend, and his mum – as they were so close to Southend seafront – ran a bed and breakfast business. In the 1950s, many residents of seafront properties sacrificed a bedroom or two in the season to supplement their incomes. Most of these establishments had linoleum on the floor – and steam radio! The first family television had to be charged up every week.

During the 1953 floods, these seafront homes became unusable, when the waters came over the sea wall right through the gasworks, taking the gasworks' waste with them, and leaving plenty of residue behind. The bed and breakfast trade was supplemented by the coaches bringing people to see the illuminations. There were so many of these coaches during the illuminations that they even parked on Southchurch Park, and if those on board lost their coach or had too much to drink, this was good news for the landladies, providing them with a lot of extra last-minute custom.

The day-tripper industry created a lot of jobs in the town in those days, and Ray felt that people were not too proud to clean toilets or work as kitchen porters, with even the elderly working as deckchair attendants. There was then an enormous casual workforce working in the amusement arcades, and doing jobs such as barkers for the coach rides for holidaymakers – rides that visited places like Canewdon, Stambridge Fisheries and Hadleigh Castle, or conducted 'mystery tours'. Pea-picking was also available on local farms.

One of Ray's jobs in the 1950s was parking bicycles at the newly opened Roots Hall stadium, at 3*d* per bike. Because just about everyone arrived on two wheels in those days, this was a very busy job, especially as kick-off approached. The car-parking area was not surfaced and the bikes were crammed in, with the large number of copper coins weighing down Ray's pockets. Motorbikes cost 6*d*, cars 5*s* and coaches 10*s*. The stadium then was pretty basic, with people standing on

Southend United Football Club programme, 1953. (Smeeton collection)

earth to watch the game. He remembers the average customer as sporting a cloth cap and a pack of five Woodbines. Such punters regularly came from east London – where Ray's own roots are – to watch Southend United, depending on whom they were playing of course. They paid around 1s 6d entrance and about 3d for a programme.

Once the wartime barbed wire was cleared from Southend seafront, it became a Londoner's paradise, with not only Roots Hall (from 1955) and the Kursaal, but kiss-me-quick amusements and a host of public houses. For residents and visitors alike, furniture and clothing were all very functional (utility), and even bicycle pedals were made of wood until into the 1950s, when aluminium meant they became much lighter. Ray himself had an ex-WD (ex-War Department) motorbike before moving on to his first car – or banger – a £5 Austin Rover Sunbeam.

In common with many people in Southend during the heyday of cinema, he was spoiled for choice in the town. He remembers that the Strand in the town centre also had live 'hocus–pocus' nights with magicians, and that the Plaza in Southchurch showed older films than the others. The New Vic in Talza Arcade had double seats upstairs for courting couples. The Regal Theatre in Tylers Avenue was the place to go if you liked something a tad more risqué, although risqué at that time was on a par with the Jane cartoons in the *Daily Mirror*, tame with hindsight. For naughty books, you were limited to naturist magazines, although Bobin's, the bookshop in Talza Arcade, did stock a few imported magazines on its top shelf. The town was even served by two local weekly newspapers then, the *Southend Standard* and the *Southend Pictorial*, which was published at the weekend.

During the 1950s, the area now known as Victoria Circus was known as Cobweb Corner because of all the trolley-bus wires. Trolley buses were known as yo-yos and were run by Southend Corporation to no apparent timetable, but operated a hop-on/hop-off circular route around the town. Bus routes were also provided by Benfleet Motors (green), Westcliff Motors (red) and the City Coach Company (chocolate brown), all of which lined up by the Talza Arcade.

Ray Davy was married at St Mary's, Prittlewell, and spent his early married life in two rooms in the family house. The couple progressed to a nearby upstairs flat, and their first mortgage was on an ex-council property in St Benet's Road, Southend, as a result of the government's occupier purchase scheme in the 1950s. His son was born in 1955 at Rochford Hospital and his daughter in 1960 at Silverdale Avenue, Westcliff, their home by that time.

As a teenager, his wife had worked in the California factory in Victoria Avenue, manufacturers of biscuits, drinks, nuts and even ice-cream. On marriage, she became a housewife. The teenage scene in the 1950s intrigued Ray, although he was not a direct part of it. He was interested to see that teenagers were finding their own style, but it was not dressing down: it was gaberdine suits with big shoulders, Prince of Wales checks, brothel creepers with crêpe soles, ox-blood winkle-pickers and slim ties. The Teddy Boy had arrived in Southend.

For the family, holidays were mainly at a caravan at Clacton, but day trips were popular from the end of the Pier utilising one of the many paddle steamers then in operation – the *Royal Sovereign*, the *Queen of Thanet*, the *Golden Eagle* and the *Royal Daffodil*, which went as far as the French coast.

Ray progressed to managing the car park at Roots Hall, following in dead man's shoes. By the end of the 1950s, the Southend United Football Supporters' Club was a prestigious organisation, one of the largest in the UK, with only Ipswich having more support. Local teams using Roots Hall included Monarch, Thorpe Athletic and Airborne, and no objections were raised about the basic facilities, especially with regard to the changing rooms.

This of course was only a sideline for Ray, albeit a very important one. His main earning power, after a stint with Southend Water, was initially with the Inland Revenue, where he started in 1948 when it was in Victoria Avenue. It then moved to Queen's Road. By the 1960s he had progressed to the National Provincial, then one of the big five national banks, as a personal taxation specialist. He remembers that his first season ticket to London from Southend Victoria was £80 per annum.

But the beautiful game always held a powerful attraction for Ray, who had thought of playing professionally at one time, and he always relished the idea that he would be able to spend more time involved with Southend United when he retired.

Round about the 1960s, Southend United had its own loan club, a prevalent culture in many pubs at the time ('winkle clubs'). For a halfpenny, or a penny, per week, people could build up their savings and draw money four times a year (quarterage) if they needed money for unexpected expenses such as funerals. From 1959, the luxury of floodlights appeared at Roots Hall. Ray cannot remember missing a single home game, at a time when even reserve games attracted a huge attendance. Early facilities at the greyhound stadium used by United before 1955 were far less satisfactory, because this was designed, obviously, for dog racing. The players had to cross a gang-plank across the greyhound track to prevent stud damage from their football boots. Although still known as the 'Greyhound' Park, the site is now a retail complex.

Other sports have played a part in Ray's life over the years – for example, cricket, when it was played at Belfairs and Chalkwell Park as well as at Southchurch Park.

The new Civic Centre (right) and concrete office blocks in Victoria Avenue, 1968. (Peter Ashton collection)

Away from sport, Ray talked about the New Year ball at the Pier pavilion, which featured big bands and big names such as Joe Loss. This was run by nurses from Southend Hospital as a fund-raiser. Billy Cotton and Henry Hall were other visitors to the dance hall. At home, Radio Caroline gradually took over from the poor reception of Radio Normandy, and things were opening up musically. His son was travelling to London by the end of the 1960s to see live groups.

In the town at this time, Ray was saddened to see the demise of the impressive Municipal College and the beautiful Clark's College near Victoria Circus (a private school), not to mention the bowling green, large houses and allotments, all of which made way for 1960s concrete and glass office blocks in Victoria Avenue.

As a popular councillor, and an adoptive Southender, his involvement with the town, and with his beloved Southend United, continues apace.

PAT DALTON

Bed, Breakfast and the Rest

Although married with two young sons, Pat was only 21 when she moved to Southend in 1950. Her father had always liked the idea of a boarding house, and this seemed the ideal opportunity for him to follow his dream, although he did not give up his day job as a machine minder/master printer for the *Sunday Pictorial* (now the *Mirror*). As a result, Pat, her husband Albert and their sons John (21 months) and Brian (5 months), her four younger brothers and their parents all moved from Kent into the roomy guest house (now the Atlantis) in Alexandra Road, opposite the bowling green. The four brothers shared attic rooms, Pat shared a large room with Albert and the boys, and the spare four bedrooms were let out on a bed and breakfast, or sometimes a full-board, basis. The house had a large garage for six cars, and renting out space could bring in 7s 6d per week, as even then there were parking problems.

Looking across the bowling green, Southend, towards the Daltons' bed and breakfast establishment in Alexandra Road. (Dalton collection)

Albert with sons John and Brian, 1951, on
Southend Pier. (Dalton collection)

Pat Dalton, Albert, John and Brian outside
the bowling green in Alexandra Road,
Southend. (Dalton collection)

The house needed a lot of work at the time, including a damp course, but Pat's dad and her husband were very hands-on in spite of their full-time jobs. Albert was a heating engineer, and later worked at the Nat West tower in London, but in the 1950s he did whatever work was available, such as painting and decorating, mostly on contracts. His father-in-law worked three nights most weeks, always including a Saturday, and, in the end, kept working until retirement.

Pat soon established a routine, working in the B&B in the mornings, an afternoon walk along the seafront while the babies had an afternoon nap, and an evening walk to see the illuminations when they were awake. As they grew older, Pat took them with her on her afternoon walks, pushing their pram to the end of the Pier on occasions, even in the rain, where with a bit of luck there would be a puppet show as a treat, but the walks were more about exercise and fresh air.

Even when they reached toddling age, they were still included in Pat's daily activities. On one afternoon walk, Brian, then 3, disappeared along the seafront, putting Pat into a panic. Thinking she could only resolve the situation if she went home for help, she found him calmly waiting for her and very proud of the fact that he knew his way home. Before this scare, Pat had a different kind of scare to contend with. In 1951 she spent some time with tuberculosis in Southend Hospital, and at the same time as she was there, 2-year-old John contracted

Pat, promoting the Rivoli cinema in the window of Norris's furniture shop, Southend High Street, 1952. (Dalton collection)

pneumonia and so he was brought in too. They were both discharged in a matter of weeks, although Pat did have surgery later.

In 1952, she worked in the Rivoli cinema in Alexandra Street (now the Empire Theatre) selling ice-creams from 7 p.m. to 9 p.m. six nights a week while Albert looked after the boys. This paid 15s per week plus 6d for every pound's worth of ice-cream sold. As ice-creams were only 6d each, this meant that Pat's total wage for the week rarely exceeded £1.

She was even persuaded by the owner of the Rivoli to take part in a publicity stunt one week to promote the current film *24 Hours of a Woman's Life*, featuring Richard Todd and Merle Oberon. For this she had to sit in the window of Norris's furniture store in Southend High Street for three-minute stretches between 2 p.m. and 4 p.m. every day for a week. If anyone saw her move within those three minutes they were awarded free tickets. Although Pat was allowed to move between the three-minute sessions, this was no easy task. There was no pay,

Pat – in a Miss Lovely bikini – and Albert decorating the steps down to the beach in Southend, west of the Pier. (Dalton collection)

either, but she did get to keep the dress, which was specially made for her at a shop in Hamlet Court Road.

Although there was not a lot of time for a social life, a friend from the Rivoli accompanied Pat on occasion to one of the big-band dances at the Kursaal. Albert would come along at the end of the evening to walk her home. Otherwise there were plenty of local pubs in which to spend a social hour or so if the opportunity presented itself.

During the summer, Pat went swimming at the open-air pool on the seafront at Westcliff, and regularly took part in the Miss Lovely competitions held every Wednesday, weather permitting. The boys would sit and watch her swimming, and then watch her parade around the deck and the pool's edge. One year she won a prize for five consecutive weeks, including second place on one occasion when the prize was Goya perfume (also-rans received prizes such as swim hats). Unfortunately, young Brian took it into his head to empty this particular bottle of perfume into the bath. A disappointing end to a moment of glory.

The bed and breakfast trade in Southend in the 1950s was a big money-spinner for the town. The Alexandra Road house already had a regular clientele, people who returned year on year for their annual fortnight's holiday; people from as far away as the Midlands and the north of England and usually, but not always, elderly. In addition, being so close to Southend Central station, it was one of the first places those holidaymakers who had not booked would stumble across. There were many hotels along Clifftown Parade, and these would pass on their overflow to the smaller units, as would the Alex in nearby Alexandra Street, then quite an upmarket hotel as well as a pub.

One particularly busy night, a couple of men who knocked on the door 'begging' for a bed were offered mattresses on the floor of the large bathroom, and accepted the offer; whether they were charged the usual B&B price of 7s 6d per night is unrecorded. What is a matter of record, however, is the fact that, in the fifteen years that the guest house continued to trade, there was no trouble in the sense of violence, vandalism or even drunkenness. By 1956, the charge had increased to £1 per night.

As full board was also on offer, there was plenty of cooking and shopping and washing up to be done. The nearest place for shopping was Schofield and Martin in Alexandra Street, near the old police station, which dealt primarily with the hotel trade and wholesalers. But the Co-op in Southchurch Road was also a regular haunt, with the staff rushing around collecting the goods you needed in the days before self-service. Pat and her mum would take Pat's large pram to carry the bulk they needed. Although rationing was still around in the early 1950s, special vouchers were available for hoteliers to buy extras such as tins of fruit. Ration books themselves were collected at Belfields School in Victoria Avenue, where the Civic Centre now stands. The Co-op, incidentally, also gave a Christmas party for local children at the Labour Hall (now the undertaker's) in Queensway, Southend.

Pat's children were taught to be especially well behaved in view of the fact that there were always guests coming and going. She feels it was a good form of discipline, and was proud of the fact that she could take them at a very young age to British Home Stores in Southend High Street for lunch (when the restaurant was on the ground floor) without having to worry about their behaviour.

They liked to visit James, the baker's on the corner of Clarence Street and the High Street, who always had broken biscuits available cheaply. John also remembers being dispatched, with young brother Brian, to buy a dozen ice-creams at Rossi's on the corner of Prittlewell Square, 200yd away. Rossi's had a restaurant and an ice-cream parlour on this site; it is now a bar. By the time they got back, the size of the ice-cream cones seemed to have diminished, thanks to some mutual licking – well, they had to stop the drips somehow. Never Never Land on the seafront was another favourite, especially in the dark when a guide would usher people around with a torch, saying 'let the kiddies in front please'.

An occasional evening treat would be to choose a trip on a charabanc from those waiting on the seafront along Eastern Esplanade. These would leave at around 7.30 p.m. and take Pat and her boys to one of the outlying villages – Rochford or Canewdon were favourites. There was no charge for the boys because of their age, and the three of them would spend a happy evening in the garden of a country pub. This was at a time when it never seemed to rain.

Every year, at carnival time, Pat entered her sons in the Beautiful Toddler competition, and Brian won second prize the first year that he went in for it (1952) in Chalkwell Park.

In the 1950s, there was a regular summer season at the bandstand in Clifftown Parade, and the orchestral concerts could be clearly heard from the back garden of the Alexandra Road house. A regular was Charlie Shadwell, and the B&B would often take in musicians from his (BBC Variety) Orchestra during the season. Pat remembers being fascinated by the oboe in particular, although she herself had been playing piano since she was 8 years old. Her dad played the violin, and her mum played the piano.

The piano was an accepted part of the furniture, and when Pat and Albert were offered a three-bedroom council house at Kent Elms, Leigh-on-Sea, in 1956, the piano went with them, and a new one was bought for the Southend house. By this time, they had another son, Paul, who was born in Rochford Hospital in 1955 but died tragically in 1957. Pat feels that this may well have been some kind of allergic reaction to an injection for whooping cough/diphtheria, but at the time his illness, and his death, which followed within days, were regarded as due to inflammation of the brain.

Pat's older boys had been going to St Helen's School, which used to be next to St Bernard's in Milton Road, Westcliff, and they continued there after their move to Leigh. Pat still used the bus on a daily basis to visit the seafront, and to help her mum out on Fridays. After school, the children would spend a bit of time with their grandparents before she collected them to take them back home.

Teresa, Pat's first daughter, was born in 1957 at home in Kent Elms, ten months before young Paul died, and Bernadette was born in 1958 at Rochford Hospital. During this period, Albert was in plumbing, heating and ventilating, although still reliant on contract work. They decided to make the financial commitment to buy their own home in Pinewood Avenue, backing onto Eastwood Park, Leigh-on-Sea, in 1961. This set them back £4 10s per week, and was a bit of a financial struggle with four children.

Soon after, the girls also started school, at Our Lady of Lourdes in Manchester Drive, Leigh. The boys were by now at St Thomas More in Kenilworth Gardens, Westcliff, and were old enough to see the girls onto the bus in the mornings, but Pat collected them all after school. Teresa, incidentally, went one better than brother Brian in 1961, when she won first prize as Fry's Turkish Delight at the annual bandstand fancy-dress competition at carnival time.

John and Brian were both boy Scouts, and both had paper rounds. Of the 7s 6d per week they received, Pat persuaded them to save 5s and the rest they could spend on pop records, progressing from a wind-up record player to a radiogram. This was, of course, the 1960s, when music tastes were changing radically. Pat did try to teach John the piano, but he was more interested in scouting at the time; Brian, however, learned to play the melodica, and the girls played recorders at school. Innovatively, the girls' school started music lessons in the mid-1960s, and they were chosen to learn violin, music to Pat's ears. Although left-handed, Teresa ended

Teresa winning first prize at the carnival fancy-dress competition, 1961. (Dalton collection: original photo Gainsborough Studio, Westcliff)

up playing violin in the Southend Youth Orchestra in the 1970s, while Bernadette turned to art.

By 1965, the bed and breakfast business in Southend was struggling, and slowly reverted to being a home rather than a business. It came in very useful for Pat's four brothers, however. All of them started married life with their grandparents in Alexandra Road, and as one moved out to his own home so the next married, until all eventually flew the nest. But every Sunday afternoon in the 1960s was a family reunion at Alexandra Road.

Southend band stage, more popularly known as the bandstand, located on the Cliffs, pre-1956. (Nicholls collection)

ALAN THURSTON

On Duty and On Stage

As a child in East Ham, Alan enjoyed boat trips to Southend-on-Sea in the *Golden Eagle*, and enjoyed holidays here in a bed and breakfast establishment in Lucy Road. Little did he know that he would be living here in the 1960s, and again in retirement.

In 1948 Alan joined the Royal Marines in preference to doing National Service, and he joined the Essex police force in 1955, the force being a magnet for many ex-servicemen. At the end of the 1950s, he was a police officer on Canvey Island, complete with bicycle, cloak, truncheon, whistle and torch. It was while on Canvey that he was first on the scene of a particularly nasty domestic murder. But most of the time he cycled backwards and forwards from The Smack to the Point, and had to be near a red telephone box every hour in case he was needed – in the absence of mobile phones.

At that time he lived in one of the police houses in Long Road, Canvey, but he had to come to Southend to give evidence and found out that the Southend force wore Horne Bros suits and received a £5 per week allowance towards rent. He was getting a bit tired of moving into different police accommodation every few years, and asked for a transfer. Luckily – in spite of a long waiting list – he got the job, and was able to purchase his first home in South Crescent, Prittlewell, in 1962. His interview with the chief constable apparently focused on his ability at football, cricket and singing (the latter for the concert party), as he already fulfilled the criteria of being 5ft 10in and ex-forces.

In fact, Alan comes from a musical family. His mum had received some musical training, and his dad played piano. As a member of the Southend concert party, he wore the blue blazer (another uniform), and enjoyed singing at the local village halls, such as Wakering. The concert party's pianist, Vera, was also involved with the Westcliff Operatic and Dramatic Society, and persuaded Alan to join, initially in the back row of the chorus. But he was then offered the opportunity to play in *Chu Chin Chow* following a conversation at an after-show party at the Grand Hotel, Leigh, and then progressed to *Oklahoma*. This, by the way, was very much in keeping with the kind of self-made and affordable entertainment that Alan still misses.

WOADS put on two musicals per year at the time. After *Oklahoma* came *Guys and Dolls*, with a small acting part (around six lines) – as a policeman, of course. The auditions were held in Prittlewell, and rehearsals were in a kind of hut next to the Blue Boar. Vera recommended that Alan try for a more significant role and he got it, as Sky Masterson. He vividly remembers first-night nerves at the idea

The police station in Alexandra Street, Southend, 1950s. (Nicholls collection)

of performing such a role on the stage of the Palace Theatre, which dissipated once he was actually on stage. During the 1960s, he feels that the Palace Theatre was always full.

For a start, his own mum would bring a charabanc from her club in east London. The mayor and mayoress would attract attention by going to the first performance and joining the cast on stage afterwards. Even Alma Cogan came to one performance, a very well-known songstress in the 1950s, and a friend of their usual director, Alexander Bridge. Unfortunately, she arrived just as Alan was in his vest, imbibing sherry during the interval, so she may not have been too impressed.

Alexander Bridge's critiques at the end of the first night were dreaded by all the actors. He sat watching at the back of the stalls and was a hard taskmaster, but he did give Alan confidence, so much so that he was happy to go for the lead again in *South Pacific* in 1965.

Alan also won a trophy or two when he took part in the talent contests that were organised annually as part of the Southend carnival. His speciality, not

Alan Thurston, his son Stephen, and two other
members of the cast of South Pacific, *1965.* (Thurston
collection)

surprisingly, was songs from the musicals of the
period. Not content with talent shows and
WOADS, Alan was part of a musical trio (with
Vera on the piano, and another singer, Betty),
which earned him around 3 guineas a performance when he could fit it in. His favourite
song at the time was 'Luck be a Lady Tonight'.
At one Masonic do, two superintendents and
the chief inspector were in the audience; what
Alan was doing was not actually condoned in
the police force, but because of the secrecy of
the Masons they could do nothing about his
moonlighting.

At the time, there were 296 police officers in the
borough of Southend. However, it was still 'villagey'
enough for the CID to phone him if there was a
burglary in his vicinity, ensuring his involvement
with the local community. This involvement – along
the lines of a village bobby – stretched to locals
knocking at his door for help to shift a dead rat or to
replace a light bulb in a lamppost.

His favourite beat, as one of the 'Borough Men', was the High Street, where
two officers patrolled one side of the railway bridge, and two the other. He got to
know local residents when they were out shopping or enjoying the seafront. Later,
there were two police cars constantly touring up and down between Pier Hill and
the Kursaal, and a police caravan was set up opposite the Kursaal so that people
could be charged before being removed to the police station. Alan also remembers
being involved in one sea rescue, when he was able to use the specially kitted-out
rescue vehicle, which carried two inflatables (one on the roof).

Overall, the traffic division in the area as far as Rayleigh Weir was very
effective. In the 1960s, mods and rockers alike were stopped when they were
heading in convoy into the town. Police cars sat on the verges of the A13 and A12
and stopped them, announcing that they wanted to check licences, insurance and
the safety of their scooters or bikes. They were told that they could turn around if
they wanted to avoid any problems, and around three-quarters of them would
promptly disappear! He cannot recall encountering any of the troubles associated
with such groups.

One incident that he recounts with some pride is when he spotted a flash of
light in a closed garage along the London Road when he was driving the duty
officer from Southend to Westcliff. The police car pulled up, and he waited at the
back entrance, the duty officer at the front. Two guys crashed out of the plate-

"SOUTH PACIFIC"

THE CHARACTERS (in order of appearance):

Ngana .... STEFANIE MITCHELL, PHOEBE SCHOLFIELD

Jerome .... ANDREW CHEESEMAN, NICHOLAS CHEESEMAN

Henry .... TONY PHILBRICK

Ensign Nellie Forbush .... ANNE HARRISON

Emile de Beque .... ALAN THURSTON

Bloody Mary .... EILEEN FARROW

Stewpot .... ANDRÉ BATLEY

Luther Bellis .... ALFRED ROPER

Professor .... DAVID WARREN

Lt. Joseph Cab'e, U.S.M.C. .... PETER EMERTON

Capt. George Brackett, U.S.N. .... LESLIE GANT

Commdr. William Harbison, U.S.N. .... NICHOLAS LOWE

Radio Operator Bob McCaffrey .... SYMON WHALVIN

Pte. Sven Larsen .... BOB LEWIS

Ensign Lisa Manelli .... PATSY O'CONNOR

Ensign Pamela Whitmore .... VALERIE CHAPMAN-SMITH

Ensign Janet McGregor .... JANET LEWIS

Ensign Bessie Noonan .... PATRICIA WATSON

Ensign Sue Yaeger .... HAZEL SINGER

Ensign Dinah Murphy .... JANET DIGBY

Liat .... MAUREEN CORBETT

Lt. Buzz Adams .... GARTH SCHOLFIELD

Native Children ..... Linda Baldwin, Lesley Simpson, Doreen Thorogood, Stephen Thurston, Tessa Walters.

Islanders, Sailors, Marines, Officers ...... Norma Burford, Irene Chesher, Naomi Conway, Jennifer Crago, Muriel Crossley, Joy Curtis, Deirdre Finch, Joyce Fugeman, Angela Harvey, Linda Heard, Daphne Lowe, Helena MacNamara, Jennifer Mentern, Doreen Philbrick, Rita Realff, Margaret Schönbeck, Pamela Sendell, Eileen Shults, Geraldine Smith, Jacqueline Smith, Susan Ward, Warwick Bain, John Bennett, Nicholas Clough, Bill Cornish, John Funnell, Douglas Robertson, Peter Roper, Stephen Roper, John Smith, Will Stewart, John Vass and Henry Whalvin.

Palace Theatre programme, 1965. (Thurston collection)

glass window at the back of the garage, and Alan managed to grab one by the collar because he had got himself stuck trying to climb over the chestnut fencing. The one he had grabbed had a back pocket full of bank notes, and although the other escaped by climbing a tree, the CID knew who he was likely to be and managed to track him down in his flat near Benfleet station. The police had limited powers of arrest outside Southend, but Alan's involvement in this case was one of many things that made the job, for him, worthwhile.

Alan was one of the traffic police on duty during the Beatles' renowned second visit to Southend at the end of 1963. Essex Police accompanied them as far as Southend, where the local force took over, clearing the way for the Fab Four in their chauffeured Rolls-Royce. The crowds near the Odeon in the High Street were held back with the help of the police on the beat, but although there was a lot of noise, and much jostling, there were no serious incidents.

The annual police ball was held at the Kursaal, paid for by the traders on the seafront in gratitude to the police. The owner of the Kursaal supported this event, which was well attended by the Watch Committee (financial watchdogs), the mayor and the chief constable. The specials were out in force while the ball was on, in the absence of police officers on the streets.

Alan married in 1952, and his three children were educated for some years in Southend as they were then at secondary level. The eldest, Stephen, went to Southend High School for Boys, and the next two, Janine and Mickey, went to Prince Avenue Juniors (near the Bell junction). The boys were in the local Scouts' troop, and Stephen turned up as one of the children in *South Pacific* at the Palace Theatre, thanks to a bit of parental influence. Alan and his wife even found time to take in foster children, mostly short term, and usually waifs and strays who had lost their families on a visit to Southend.

By 1966, the writing was on the wall for the Borough Men, who were being absorbed into Essex Police. Although Alan and his colleagues were told they could stay (as long as they did not want promotion), he decided it was time to move on, and the family moved to Hounslow to do something completely different – run a successful Tupperware business. But when it was time to retire, he came back, and takes great pleasure in once again living in the town.

DANNY ROWE

A Nursing Life

Born in Thorpe Bay in 1930, Danny spent the best part of her working life in Southend as a nurse. She began her SRN training at Rochford Hospital in 1948, her first time away from home, where she had lived with her divorced mother and her maternal grandparents.

Initially, she had thought about physiotherapy as a career when she left St Bernard's in Milton Road, Westcliff, but she was not old enough for that at 18, so planned to spend one year in nursing, which turned into rather longer than that. Rochford General Hospital was then an established training school, and remained a separate entity from Southend Hospital until the early 1960s.

All the trainee nurses lived in, and were only allowed out late – that is, after 10 p.m. – on one day per month. Students worked shifts, with the day duty finishing around 9 p.m. giving them time to sign in by the 10 p.m. deadline, which would be checked on a daily basis by the home sister. The day shift started at 7.30 a.m. with a few hours off in the afternoon, giving a working week of fifty-two hours. Additionally, Danny had twenty-four months of night duty (9 p.m. to 8 a.m.) during her four years' training.

Her first month's pay packet was £3 19s 6d and, out of their salaries, the girls had to buy their own stockings and study books. Trainees came from all over the world, applying directly to the hospital – Irish girls featured particularly strongly, but there were also African girls and a couple from countries such as Czechoslovakia.

Although Rochford Hospital did not have a casualty unit, as A&E was then known, it did have an emergency reception. In fact, it was while Danny was on reception one November evening that she recalls a gentleman collapsing at her feet, having driven himself from Hockley in spite of being badly burned as a result of lighting his bonfire with paraffin.

The hospital building was a former workhouse, an old red-brick structure (demolished and replaced with housing in the 1990s) with large ponds in the grounds, and wards named after local notables such as Herbert Dowsett (former Southend mayor and JP). The Care of the Elderly Unit was one of the largest units, with four wards, and there were two thirty-six-bed TB wards.

Three months were spent at the Primary Teaching School before the trainees progressed onto the wards. Danny's first ward practice was on the Gynaecological Ward, and this became her favourite, along with midwifery. It was also a bit of an eye-opener. When one patient asked Danny for a fanny frock, she had no idea that she was referring to a sanitary towel.

Danny Rowe at the July 1952 prize-giving when she was awarded a bronze medal for a 75 per cent pass in theory and practical nursing. (Rowe collection)

Exams were held annually (or sometimes more often) at Oldchurch Hospital, Romford, covering all nursing practices including orthopaedics, geriatrics, bandaging, theatre, maternity and gynaecology, and the finals (written and practical) were taken in Rochford Hospital after three years. The day Danny took her written finals was the day King George died, and the day of her practical exam was the day he was buried, both in 1952.

During her training, Danny got involved in organising dances at summer and Christmas in the nurses' home for the Student Nurses' Association. They could afford to hire a small band by selling tickets, but were invariably short of men. On one occasion Danny asked a friend to bring some extra men, and this was how she came to meet Jim, who worked in shipping in London. They became engaged before she passed her finals, to the apparent disgust of Matron, who phoned her mother to suggest that Danny was 'wasting her training'. All the matrons that Danny recalls at the time were single, and none of them was ever that happy with married ladies working.

It was not just difficult for the students to meet boyfriends; conducting a relationship – however innocent – was also hard work. Men friends were only allowed as far as the first-floor sitting room, and this was strictly controlled. To escape on a date, Danny would have to employ such manoeuvres as waiting for an ambulance to arrive so that she could slip out through the gate, although Jim did discover a lower part of the wall that he could step over. An occasional treat was to be allowed to stay at her own home overnight on a Saturday after duty, and on such evenings she and Jim would treat themselves to an evening dancing at the Kursaal to a live band, an occasion that merited dressing up. It seems, if Danny remembers correctly, that the Kursaal actually laid on a late-night bus to take people home at the end of the evening.

They married in 1952 at St Saviour's in King's Road, Leigh. The reception was held at the White Hall in Chesterfield Crescent, Eastwood. Danny's mum was a dressmaker, which enabled her to work from home and therefore look after her ageing parents. Mum was also wardrobe mistress with the Southend Operatic and Dramatic Society for a number of years. So it was Mum who made Danny's

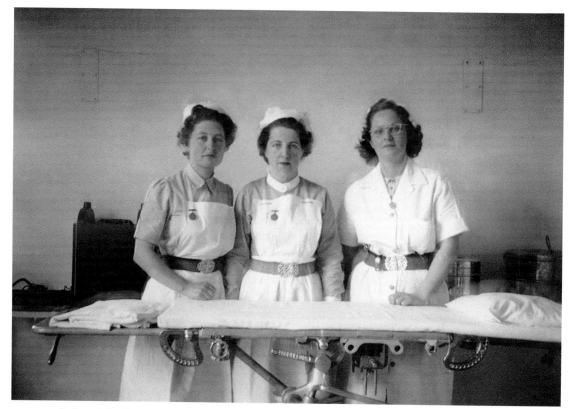

Left to right: Doreen Sporle, staff nurse, Doreen Ford, ward sister, and Danny, 1953. (Rowe collection)

elaborately beaded dress – which she still (amazingly) possesses – and those of the bridesmaids. The honeymoon was spent touring Devon and Cornwall by car, and the couple came back with just half a crown left between them.

Their first home was in Carlton Avenue, in a house that had enough outside space for growing vegetables and for keeping chickens during a time when eggs and meat were still rationed.

Passing her final exams meant that Danny could apply for a staff nurse position, via the matron. She applied first for Female Surgical, and had moved on to Male Medical by the time of the 1953 floods. Rochford Hospital took many of the bodies into their mortuary, and nurses put in extra hours to deal with people suffering from pneumonia, exposure and a whole range of injuries. Danny remembers looking out from Hadleigh Castle to the swirl and surge of the surrounding floodwater as it started to recede.

As she was now married, she took the opportunity to apply for a part-time staff nurse position at Southend Hospital, partly because it was her favourite ward: Gynaecological. This meant a different uniform, but the ward had the luxury of its own operating theatre.

In 1956, Danny left to have Gillian, and Alison followed in 1959. Both daughters were born at Rochford Hospital. Her consultant on both occasions was Miss Whapham, a former colleague.

At home, funds ran to an early washing machine and Hoover, with a television bought by her mum at the time of the coronation. The large Silver Cross pram had room enough for both babies and the family dog. Although Danny had always had a pushbike, she now took to walking everywhere with the pram, such as to her mother in Westcliff, and to friends in Leigh. Occasionally they made the slightly longer trip to Thorpe Bay to her mother's beach hut. There was also the opportunity to do some nursing practice, teaching in the evenings for the Red Cross.

Innovatively, Danny and Jim bought a plot of land in Westcliff that a friend of her mother's had been using as an allotment up until 1960. Her cousin, an architect, designed a house for them; planning consent seems to have been a breeze, building started in March and they moved in during July – and are still there.

A few years later, Danny bumped into Southend Hospital's assistant matron when walking back home after taking her children to Earl's Hall School. It appeared that the Gynaecological Ward was desperate for staff, so she agreed to go back for a fortnight – and stayed thirty-nine years. The arrangement suited her, because she was able to make special arrangements to take school holidays as unpaid leave, and work school hours during term time.

The two girls moved on to Belfairs School after their eleven-plus exams, and got involved in a number of extra-curricular activities. There were the Girl Guides, elocution lessons, horse-riding, and dancing in particular. The latter saw them as members of Mrs Wheeler's dancing school, appearing at the Palace Theatre in Christmas pantomimes such as *The Sleeping Beauty* and *The Nutcracker*, with proud Mum in the audience, of course.

Alison was the first girl in her class to have a foreign holiday when the family went from Southend airport to southern Italy in about 1967 for two weeks. There was a storm on the way back, which delayed the flight, and the aeroplane seemed exceptionally unstable and noisy to Danny during the homeward journey, especially in the loo.

As for Jim, time away from work gave him the opportunity to play football for the Southend Old Collegians, cricket for the Leigh Cricket Club (at Chalkwell Park) and squash. Danny's closest involvement with sport was to do the cricket teas at Chalkwell Park, taking the girls along when they were babies.

ERNIE HALTON

A TA Influence

Born in Leigh-on-Sea in 1931, by 1950 Ernie was doing National Service, and his sister Jean was working as a shop assistant. While he was away, his parents moved house from their council home in Croft Close, Leigh-on-Sea, to one in Bellhouse Lane that featured two loos – although he admits that one was outside the kitchen door. The rooms in the new house were spacious, wallpapered and well lit, and the lounge had a tiled surround that fronted a coal fire that heated a back-boiler, resulting in a supply of hot water. Temperature levels in winter were boosted by paraffin heaters. The kitchen sported a butler sink, but all the downstairs rooms had floors of a hard, brittle substance that did not lend itself to fixing carpets, and the windows had iron 'Crittall' frames that seemed to encourage condensation.

Ernie's mother's pride and joy were the red quarry tiles in the hall, leading from the kitchen to the front door. These were polished every day except Sunday, when she went to Belfairs Methodist Church across the road. Mum also spent time in her small back garden with its postage-stamp lawn. There she grew her Peace roses, her London Pride harebells, sweet peas and dahlias. Dad built a low brick wall to divide the lawn from the vegetable patch, where he was in charge of the potatoes, cauliflowers, runner beans, peas, carrots and beetroot.

Both parents worked at this time – Dad as a building maintenance worker, and Mum doing housework for a lady in Eastwood Road. As for Ernie, he was demobbed in August 1951 and then obliged to serve three years with the Territorial Army, this technically forming part of his five-year service overall.

With the TA he trained as a radar operator on equipment sited at the TA premises in Eastwood Road North (opposite the Woodcutter's Arms), and was subsequently promoted to the rank of bombardier. The CO (Major 'Toby' Westoby) presumed on his friendship with the manager of the Kursaal by calling on his expertise to construct the decorations that were used at the TA's drill hall monthly dances. These were not cheap hops, to use Ernie's description, as all the TA members were required to wear their best blue uniforms and the guests were admitted by ticket only, and were required to wear evening dress. On one particular occasion, the Dutch ambassador was one of the invited guests and the hall was decorated with a Dutch theme. TA members not in possession of 'best blues' served as bar staff or cloakroom attendants. The dancing was to the music supplied by a band, often such as Kenny Baker, putting the dances on a par with those held at the Kursaal.

The TA 1953 carnival float about to start off in Leigh. Ernie Halton is on the float, on the left, with Shirley standing, also on the left. (Halton collection: original photo Photo-Flash, Wickford)

During this period, Ernie was part of the guard of honour that lined the London route of the funeral cortège of King George VI in 1952. A salute had to be mastered for this event, which was executed by troops only at the funeral of royalty, culminating in the muzzle of the rifle being placed on the toecap of the left boot – with disastrous results to the highly 'bulled' (polished) surface that had been achieved by many hours of spit and polish.

The following year, Ernie's TA unit was able to respond rapidly early in the morning following the Canvey Island floods, using their own transport and shovels to fill sandbags as quickly as they could. He remembers the cold and the mud underfoot while they worked non-stop until nightfall, when they were relieved by another group of volunteers, enabling Ernie and his friends to return home, tired and saddened.

Just a few months later, the unit entered a float in the Southend carnival, a scratch entry assembled just hours before the start of the Saturday procession. The theme was Achievement, and the float was built on a 3-ton Army lorry, piled with ashes from the drill hall coke boiler. On top of the heap stood the sergeant major dressed in cricket whites, with Ernie and his friend Ken in khaki battledress and tin hats standing guard with fixed bayonets on their rifles. The slogan, penned by Ernie, was:

England won The Ashes
Hillary climbed The Hill
Gordon won The Derby
The TA know their Drill.

(References here are to Edmund Hillary, Mount Everest and Gordon Richards, the jockey.) Other uniformed TA members carried tin hats in which the viewing public was invited to place and/or throw coins. There were times when these helpers wished they had worn their helmets, and Ernie and Ken were very glad they wore theirs to protect them from indiscriminately aimed coins.

The year 1953 was also when the regiment took part in the coronation celebrations held at the old Southend stadium, then the home ground of the Southend United Football Club. The TA's contribution to the 'show' was a simulated attack by American Indians on a wagon and the subsequent arrival of the American cavalry. His wife-to-be, Shirley, was one of the females rescued by the US cavalry (Ernie among them) from the covered wagon as it was attacked by the redskins.

As a staunch supporter of the Rayleigh Rockets speedway team, Ernie watched them race every Saturday evening, having cycled to the event. At one meeting, the

management of the speedway club's girl supporters challenged the girls of the TA to a netball match during the midway interval of the meeting. Ernie and Ken volunteered to accompany the TA netball team to the meeting, and this is how Ernie and Shirley met up, she being a member of the Rockets netball team. The team were invited to one of the monthly dances held at the Territorial Drill Hall, and, initially, it was Ken and Shirley who got together. For twelve months, Ernie played gooseberry to Ken and Shirley, the three of them going to dances together. But when Ernie acquired a James 197cc Captain motorbike in 1954, he

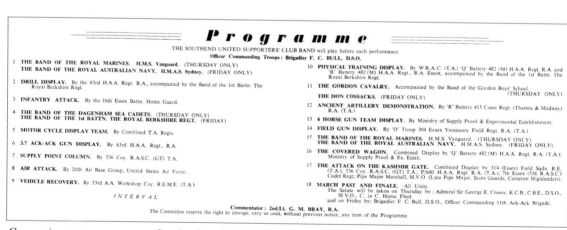

Coronation tattoo programme, Southend stadium, 1953. (Halton collection)

was able to give Shirley a lift home to Leigh-on-Sea after an evening at the Kursaal ballroom listening to Geraldo and his orchestra. Ken took off alone on his bicycle, and this gave Shirley the opportunity to confess that it was Ernie who was her favourite.

Ernie had managed to make such an impressive purchase as the motorbike as a result of moving jobs. He had been working as a plumber's mate after National Service, but found a better-paid position with E.K. Cole in Southend, using a heated press to turn out plastic components for radio valve bases, handles for steam irons, and even lavatory seats. By 1954, he was working for a furniture manufacturer on the A127, but Shirley, now that they were engaged, persuaded him to find more secure employment, and he found a clerical post with one of Lord Vestey's London companies. His was a large concern, with meat produce as its primary stock-in-trade – Sainsbury's and Dewhurst's butcher's, cattle farms overseas, plus meat producers and even the Blue Star Shipping Line. Shirley was also working in London, for a French bank.

Commuting by steam train from Southend to Fenchurch Street was not the most passenger friendly of experiences, especially in winter without any heating. Ernie recollects one journey when he fell asleep while in a window seat, and found his hair frozen to the glass when he awoke.

During the early 1950s, both Shirley and Ernie were keen supporters and members of the TA's sports facilities of netball, hockey and badminton clubs. They then joined the Methodist church (now demolished) in York Road, Southend, which had a snooker club in the basement, and where Ernie instituted a church badminton club.

As a couple, they enjoyed the huge choice of films then available in and around Southend, and they favoured traditional jazz, attending concerts at the Kursaal given by bands such as Kenny Ball, Acker Bilk or Jack Parnell, using Ernie's precious motorbike to travel around. However, Shirley's mother was their chauffeur for longer trips to see relatives, and she gave Ernie his first driving lessons in her Morris 10.

Shirley and Ernie were married at Southend register office in March 1955. A small, quiet wedding, it was attended only by close family and friends, with a reception at Shirley's home. While they were posing for photographs at the reception, the photographer asked for one with them toasting each other. Ernie's mother jumped up to get the drinks, and returned with what Ernie and Shirley thought to be glasses of gin. But one sip later, and they knew they were toasting each other in tap water. Never mind, it looked just fine in the photograph.

After a honeymoon in Cheddar, they settled with Shirley's mother in her bungalow in Eaton Road, Leigh. Their two daughters – Kim and Linda – were born in 1957 and 1958, so they moved to a rented flat above Sainsbury's butcher's in Southend High Street, provided by Ernie's employers. This flat had a large lounge overlooking the street, two bedrooms, a kitchen, bathroom and toilet. Access was via two flights of stairs, the first outside, the second inside, but the couple managed this minor inconvenience even after the birth of their son, Keith, in 1959, though it became a bit of a struggle with pram and pushchairs to get to the seafront or to the grandparents in Leigh, which involved a bus journey.

Ernie and Shirley toasting their wedding day in water, 1955. (Halton collection: original photo Carlton Studios, Westcliff)

They lived there until 1966, when, while they were on holiday in Dublin, they received a message from a neighbour to tell them they had been offered a council house but they had to accept the offer straight away. Although they curtailed their holiday, they lost out on this house. However, they were offered another in Broomfield Road, Leigh, soon after, alleviating their disappointment. This became the family home until Shirley's untimely death in 2002.

The move to Broomfield meant that the three children changed primary schools, from Porter's Grange in Southend to Blenheim School in Leigh. Ernie also changed jobs around this time, moving to the International Wool Secretariat, again in London. Another change was to transfer their church membership to the Belfairs Methodist Church in Eastwood Road North. Ernie, with help, formed another badminton club, and Shirley started a craft club. Both still exist. They also became uniformed officers of, respectively, the Boys' Brigade and the Girls' Brigade at Belfairs Church. All three children joined the brigades.

Shirley did not return to work until 1968, as her whole day was taken up with the children, although the grandparents were very obliging babysitters. She worked as a cashier for Cater's, a small supermarket in Southend High Street. The family had no transport until 1972, when they bought a Ford Anglia car. In the meantime, weekends were spent in visiting both sets of grandparents, who lived within walking distance. Holidays were spent in and around the Southend area – and why not.

EVELYN CLINE

Youth Mayor

Evelyn is Southend born and bred. She lived with her parents and younger brother in Royston Avenue in the 1950s, when the area was very rural. When she was a teenager, Evelyn's life revolved around the many local youth clubs and the church. In fact, in 1951 she was elected (by members of the youth clubs) the first youth mayor for the Southend area. A memorable moment for Evelyn was being presented with her chain of honour by Canon Ellis Gowing. She retained the role until 1953, the year of the coronation, when her duties took her to London with invitations to a ringside seat in Parliament Square, tea at Lambeth Palace with Princess Margaret, and a special service at Westminster Abbey.

Locally, her involvement with the youth centres meant that she organised sporting activities such as football, netball, table tennis and basketball. Later, when she was warden of Shoebury Youth Centre, she had ex-Southend professional footballers Jack French and Frank Dudley as assistant wardens. Before that she had a stint as warden of Focus Youth Centre in Southend, and she also organised a monthly fund-raising ball at the Pier pavilion. These dances were big-band events, with the girls in long evening dresses and most of the men in dinner suits, and were open to anyone under 21.

From 1949 to 1959 Evelyn commuted to London to her job as a stenographer, working for two different employers during that time. The Fenchurch Street line prior to 1953 was served by steam trains, and she frequently arrived at work with soot on her face, hair and clothes, so that the clothes had to go to the dry cleaners on Friday on a regular basis. She also remembers the dramatic effect that the 1953 floods had on the trains, the bus service replacing them for quite a long time.

At the time of the floods, her father was manager of Maxwell's (the owners of Peter Pan's playground on the seafront) with an office on the Pier. Peter Pan's itself was under water after the floods hit, and he went to the Pier to see what he could rescue. After poking his head through a broken window to survey the damage, he brought it out again a bit too sharply, and ended up with a very nasty gash across his skull. Evelyn can recall free bags of coal being handed out along the seafront to those affected, to help them to dry out their saturated homes.

After church on Sundays, Evelyn and her friends would meet up at Tomassi's, when it was on the opposite side of Southend High Street. Hot chocolate was the favoured tipple, and the venue had the ambience of a coffee bar, with only the jukebox missing. Even more memorable perhaps were the ballroom-dancing lessons she had at Mimi Green's dance studio in London Road, Westcliff, because

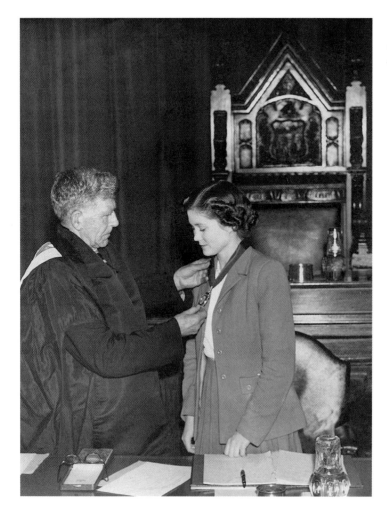

Evelyn Cline receiving her youth council badge of office from Canon Gowing, 1952. (Cline collection)

this is where she met her husband, Geoffrey. Geoffrey became a public health officer and worked locally in environmental health for many years.

They married in 1958 at St Mary's, Prittlewell, and had their reception at the Castle Hotel on the seafront. This was a sit-down turkey dinner for 126 people. As a typical wedding prank, some of their friends locked them in the train carriage after the reception when they were making their way from Southend East to Westcliff station, and they had to tip the porter to open it up for them so they could get out. Their wedding present from Geoffrey's parents was the deposit on a house in Sutton Road – the house where Evelyn still lives. She was carried over the threshold in her wedding dress. Other wedding presents included deckchairs, a Lloyd Loom stool and a pouffe (their only furniture initially apart from a bed and the kitchen table and chairs), plus a pressure cooker, a colander and a cake stand. They went on honeymoon to Ostend from Southend airport in a tiny scheduled aircraft, and were the only two people on board what seems to have been a bit of a bumpy ride.

Evelyn and her brother Terry at a 1950s youth ball at the Pier pavilion. (Cline collection)

For Evelyn, the 1960s were spent bringing up her children, Lynda (born 1959), Malcolm (1961) and Zena (1967), with Trevor coming along in 1970. Lynda was born in an upstairs bedroom, the others in the downstairs dining room, with home births being favoured by Evelyn primarily as a result of a newspaper report in the late 1950s that identified a case of babies being mixed up in Rochford Hospital, which obviously worried her.

Both sets of grandparents were a great help financially to Evelyn and Geoffrey. Her parents bought their first pram, and his parents bought most of the remaining baby equipment. Evelyn used a Flatley drier to dry nappies, which had an electric element in the base, and was very popular among young mums.

The children were schooled at Wimborne Road until the age of 6, and then went to St Mary's (the same school Evelyn herself had attended). They came home for lunch, as did Geoffrey, and he was there in the evenings when Evelyn got a part-time job working at the Shoebury Centre. Southend High Street figured in daily life quite a bit. There were visits to Waitrose, which was opposite the current Royals development, to Joe Lyons on Saturday mornings with the babies (where Marks & Spencer is now), and to the health clinic in Warrior Square.

Each child was lucky enough to have an increase in pocket money every time someone in the family had a birthday – an increase of 2*d* every time. Other treats included the hire of a beach hut at Shoebury (near what is now known as Uncle Tom's Cabin) during the May half-term – not to mention the annual box at the Palace Theatre in Westcliff to see the Christmas pantomime, an occasion when the children were allowed to bring along their friends. The children also filled many of their leisure hours with local Cubs and Brownies activities.

The 1960s did not start too well for Evelyn, because her eldest daughter, Lynda, developed whooping cough and spent time in the Balmoral isolation hospital, which was then in Westcliff. Happier memories of the 1960s are of her continued involvement in the youth movement. Evelyn became a trampoline coach at Shoebury Youth Centre, achieving a professional qualification, and this

St. Mary's Parish Church, Prittlewell

The Marriage of

Evelyn Isabel Quantrill

and

Geoffrey Leonard Cline

Saturday, 9th August, 1958

Evelyn and Geoffrey wed at St Mary's in 1958. (Cline collection)

Order of service at the 1958 wedding. (Cline collection)

was the only time she ever wore trousers, for obvious reasons. During 1968 – the year of the Mexico Olympic Games – Evelyn particularly remembers the Youth Centre float at the carnival because it had a boat on it, emphasising the sporting culture of the local youth population, although it also had a very Mexican emphasis to reflect the spirit of the Games.

Three other things from the 1960s seem to have stuck in Evelyn's mind. First, a firework display at the greyhound stadium in Sutton Road in 1963, which seemed to 'celebrate' the Great Train Robbery. Secondly, her close-up view of the Queen Mother when she came to Southend officially to open the Civic Centre in 1967. The Cline family's car had been held up in Progress Road at the approach of the royal cavalcade, and the two cars were just inches apart at one point. Lots of make-up and jewellery were apparently in evidence. Lastly, her driving lessons with a Thorpe Bay instructor, who enabled her to pass first time and switch from a Vespa to four wheels.

JOHN LEWINDON

Carnival Time

John is a Southender by adoption and by commitment. He has lived in the area since he first had digs in Westcliff in the 1950s, having spent holidays here prior to that period. Although he was then working as an accountant in London, his commitment to the local community started with appearances in a few amateur productions with the Cornhill Players, who were very short of male actors at the time (1954) and asked him to step into the breach. There was a photograph of him in the *Southend Standard*, 2 December 1954, appearing in *High Spirits* as PC Mervyn Swallow.

This seems to have established an interest in the theatre and in the theatrical. As a volunteer he was very involved in the preparations for August carnival weeks in 1955 and 1957 in particular. In fact, he took his two weeks' annual holiday at carnival time, to spend one week before the carnival helping with the preparations, and one week 'on duty' at the carnival itself.

The preparations were far more spontaneous and, perhaps, manic than they are today. The 150 or so girls who entered the Carnival Queen competition at the Palace ballroom appeared on stage for the first time at 2 p.m. on the Friday, the day before the carnival, to start the process of choosing the queen and princesses. Around 130 spectators attended the start of the eliminations, utilising free tickets that were not at all easy to come by. Rank starlets of the likes of Michael Medwin and Jill Ireland were called on to interview the girls on stage as they paraded in their finery. The contestants had to be over 21, born in the borough of Southend, and available for all the appearances required of them during carnival week. At this stage, you could bet half a crown (or whatever you liked) on the winner.

At 5 p.m. eight girls were selected for the final at the Odeon in Southend High Street, which started at 7 p.m. The 3,500 tickets for this event (at 4s each) were sold out over a month in advance. These tickets had a voting form attached, so that the eight could be whittled down to six. Of these six, the one with the most votes would be crowned queen, the next would be chief maid of honour, and the other four runners–up were princesses. The two girls who just missed the final six 'titles' were standbys for appearances during the following year, as the six girls could not all commit to all the events they would be required to attend.

The evening would be kicked off with a ten–minute organ introduction, then the girls would parade in day dresses. The Sea Scouts collected the voting forms in their hats and took them to the Victor Sylvester dance studios over the foyer, with thirty tellers waiting to sort and count them. While the counting took place, the audience were treated to *Movietone News*, then a cartoon, and then a film specially released before its London run, which usually featured whatever starlet had been involved in the judging. Behind the screen, everything was happening. About sixty members of the local operatic societies (Leigh, Westcliff, Southend) would be rehearsing the crowning ceremony, and dressmakers would be working on last-minute adaptations – if necessary – of the newly bought court dresses to make sure that they fitted the lucky winners.

After the interval, the stage was set for the crowning ceremony, and, as the announcements were made, the queen, wearing her chain of office, and her court were duly honoured. The queen was given the arm of Alderman Teddy Longman, the chair of carnival during the 1950s and 1960s, and paraded down the red carpeted stairs into the foyer, followed by her courtly procession. The High Street would be closed to traffic for the occasion, and there were three lines of national press photographers waiting outside the Odeon to snap the queen getting into her carnival car and driving off. This would be about 10.30 on the Friday evening, and the photographs would be in the national, not just the local, press on Saturday morning. The court's first function would be at 10.30 a.m. on Saturday at the tiny tots parade at Chalkwell Park, with the main procession starting several hours later, covering Marine Parade, Leigh-on-Sea, to the Kursaal in Southend.

John himself was busy out selling programmes advertising carnival week. These cost half a crown, which included a tear-out voucher to win an EKCO television. With others he worked in Southend High Street on Saturday morning, and, after being provided with lunch at the Kursaal, he was driven to Leigh-on-Sea for the start of the carnival. In fact, the owner of the Kursaal at the time, C.J. Morehouse, fed all the carnival workers for the whole week.

The carnival set off promptly at 3 p.m., preceded by the F.A. Jones pantechnicon with its mobile office. Then came Captain Barton (ex-Army) in full regalia on his horse, although the police took over in later years. By 5.30 the carnival had reached the Kursaal car park, at which time the money collected en route was cashed up in the Kursaal treasury, with the money for programmes sold by John and his colleagues fully accounted for. Dinner, with wine, was provided in the rather grand Kursaal staff canteen.

John was then busy selling raffle tickets until 11 p.m. This annual raffle was for a car, and became so popular that coaches would arrive with lists of people not even on the coach but wanting to buy a raffle ticket, lists that John had to enter methodically on the ticket stubs. A lot of time during carnival week was spent by John and other volunteers selling these tickets, the car being donated by a different dealer each year. Every day – except Sunday, a free day – they were provided with clean white overalls to make them recognisable to punters wishing to try their luck. At the end of the first Saturday, John and his friends would return to Harry's Bar within the Kursaal, with its unlimited free bar, until around 2 a.m., when they would eat at Jerry's Nosh on the seafront.

Carnival Monday and Tuesday featured a children's talent show at the band-stage in Southend-on-Sea. Auditions were held over a month-long period at the Argyll Methodist Church Hall nearby, and there was a lot of rivalry between the local dancing schools to see who would win the most prizes. John showed his versatility here by doing make-up for the children taking part, working from around 2 p.m. through until 10 p.m. Volunteers were ready to change duties at a moment's notice depending on where most help was required, and this could include a stint at the Chalkwell fête, which ran every day until 10.30 p.m., except Sunday.

On Wednesday, there was the midweek carnival procession which ran from Clifftown Road to the Kursaal at 2 p.m. then back to Chalkwell Shelter along the seafront. Thursday saw John back on car ticket sales or in the carnival's offices in the morning, and at the dog show in the afternoon at Priory Park if he was needed. That evening there was a firework display either at the greyhound stadium or at Roots Hall (depending on the year). Friday was the Beautiful Toddler competition at the Kursaal. Saturday was the children's fancy dress at Southend band-stage with entertainment in the afternoon from the talent contest winners and the finale – the evening procession.

This last day of the carnival was busy with car ticket sales, with coaches and buses bringing people from as far as London and Chelmsford, all seemingly wanting to buy tickets. The ticket-sellers were taken back to the Kursaal in shifts for their lunch, and trayloads of cold drinks were supplied by Morehouse. John was also busy shaking a collecting tin at the evening illuminated procession, which ran from Chalkwell Esplanade to the Kursaal, ending up back in Harry's Bar for more refreshments until the early hours, when Morehouse himself would throw a party at his home.

In the meantime, the carnival queen was busy visiting all parts of the borough, plus the hospital, often on her 'personal' float. There was a dance for her to attend every night of carnival week, with differing venues and visiting bands, including the Dagenham Girl Pipers one year and the Vancouver Boys' Band, which were popular enough to be booked for two years. Then there was the queen of queens' dance on the final Saturday evening at the Kursaal, with visiting carnival queens from all parts of Essex, and from much further afield – as far as the Isle of Wight.

Next morning at 11 a.m. there was a Sunday thanksgiving service, attended yet again by the queen of the carnival and by John and other volunteers, and with all denominations present, including the local rabbi. This was the official end to carnival week, although there was still some work to be done in sorting out prizes. The draw for the car took place in October at the Kursaal every year, but when a 'skill' factor was brought into force in the 1960s this particular raffle was killed off. Guessing the number of balloons did not have that same element of chance somehow.

John was single and in his 20s at the time, and was quite happy to get the occasional phone call during the year asking him to sell raffle tickets for other fund-raising events. The money he raised over the years was all for local charities and to run the carnival estate, the carnival office being open for part of each week every week of the year. He also became involved in helping out at the Palace Theatre, mainly backstage and usually for pantomime or dancing-school productions. One of his favourite memories of the Palace is of Sunday afternoons

The cast of Humpty Dumpty *at the Palace Theatre, Westcliff, 1956. Hugh Lloyd as Muddles (spotted shirt), Jerry Jerome as the dame (in white apron), and Roberta Pett (Mrs Jerry Jerome) in the feathered hat. (Lewindon collection: original photo Gainsborough Studios, Westcliff)*

CLIFFS PAVILION
SOUTHEND-ON-SEA

Licensee and General Manager: H. J. POINTER, F.I.M.Ent.

For the Season—27th JUNE to 17th SEPTEMBER
Mon.–Fri. 7.45 p.m.; Sat. 6 & 8.30 p.m.; Wed. Mat. 3 p.m.
RICHARD STONE presents
THREE ENTIRELY DIFFERENT SHOWS

All with resident stars

RAWICZ AND LANDAUER

GORDON & BUNNY JAY – BRUCE ALLAN
JOANNE MICHELLE – THE CHARLETONS
CLIFFS PAVILION LOVELIES

From 27th June   "THE JULY SHOW"
Guest Star

LESLIE CROWTHER

From 25th July   "THE AUGUST SHOW"
Guest Stars

THE THREE MONARCHS

From 22nd August   "THE FINALE SHOW"
Guest Star

DAVE ALLEN

Prices   **8/6**   **7/6**   **6/6**   **5/-**   4

Wednesday Matinee, all seats 4/-

Box Office open daily 10 a.m. to 8 p.m. (including Sundays)   Telephone Southend 47382

ALL SEATS BOOKABLE   ★   ★   ★   SPECIAL RATES FOR PARTIES

—   —   —   —   POSTAL BOOKING SLIP   —   —   —   —

To The Manager, Cliffs Pavilion, Southend-on-Sea. 1966

Enclosed is cheque postal order money order value £   :   :   and stamped addressed envelope

Please send me the following tickets (please indicate clearly date, which performance, price and part of theatre required)

NUMBER OF TICKETS	DATE	PRICE	PART OF THEATRE	PERFORMANCE

NAME ....

ADDRESS ....

Printed for Southend-on-Sea Corporation by G. Taylor & Co. (Printers) Ltd., Southend-on-Sea   4000 9 66

Cliffs Pavilion flyer, 1966. (Smeeton collection)

Kursaal flyer at the 1967 carnival, Southend seafront. (Peter Ashton collection)

with Eric Easton and his electric organ, a singalong with questions, which meant that the audience could get involved in the proceedings. Additionally, John worked part-time for Southend Corporation as part of the stage staff of the Pier pavilion. They would ring up when they needed a scene shifter, but by the late 1950s non-union staff were less welcomed. Luckily, they all had other jobs – from milkman to baker to grave-digger.

By the late 1950s John was working in Southend and he married in 1959. His eldest daughter was born in 1962. His involvement by this time was rather different. He now made sure he saw every variety show at the Palace Theatre and every summer show at the Cliffs Pavilion from 1964, and he remembers seeing Leslie Crowther, Dickie Henderson, Arthur Brough and Bill Treacher (Pauline's husband in *EastEnders*) when he was a 'romantic' lead. Another memory is of seeing such touring acts as a magic show that featured the apparent slicing of a tongue. John's children did not miss out either, as they were taken along to the first of the then twice-nightly shows as soon as they were old enough.

GRAHAM SARGENT

'Evening All'

Graham Sargent was brought up in Hawkwell and lived at home with his mum, dad and brother until his marriage in 1955. His grandparents lived in Potash Cottage in Hawkwell, still there as a local feature. Although Southend was on his doorstep, a trip to the town by bus was, in itself, a holiday during his childhood, as was a trip to Hockley Woods.

It was while he was at Rayleigh Secondary School (now Fitzwimarc) in the early 1950s that he met his wife, Shirley, who lived on Canvey Island. He remembers cycling every day to Canvey to see her. But after the floods in 1953, her family moved to Hornchurch. When the couple left school, Shirley worked in London as a typist, and Graham became a trainee chef at the Abercorn Rooms, Liverpool Street. He recalls using the steam trains, which, if his memory serves him correctly, were more reliable – and even quicker – than they are half a century later. Admittedly, they were less comfortable, utilising bench seats facing each other, with no corridors or washroom facilities. The regulars in his carriage played cards on the way to work, spreading themselves out to the irritation of other passengers. There were also 'ladies only' carriages, and third-class carriages. He also remembers seeing the Britannia locomotive 'coaling up' for the journey from Liverpool Street to Norwich.

Graham's National Service intervened from 1953 to 1955, although he was based not too far away, in Colchester. As a member of the catering corps, he cooked for Major General Bower and his family. The Major General's wife was a member of the (royal) Bowes-Lyon family. This pulled in a wage of £1 8s per week, but he benefited from extra annual leave: although he was a private, he had the same annual holiday allowance as his boss. On one occasion he was put on a charge for being late back, and fined £1 – a large chunk of his wages – but it transpired that the major was not such a bad sort after all, as he gave him the £1 to pay the fine.

While in Colchester, he had just half a day off a week in which he was able to visit Shirley, even after they were married in 1955. The wedding took place in Hornchurch, their honeymoon in Torquay, and they started married life in a flat in Southend Road, Rochford, owned by an old aunt who lived downstairs. They turned the upstairs boxroom into a kitchen, but Graham had to take care with his DIY skills as his Uncle Bert was a master carpenter and did not approve of such antics as painting the natural wood (bright yellow, as it happens).

After National Service, Graham applied to join the Southend Police, and in the few months in between he worked at Trueforms shoe shop in Southend High

Street. Shirley, in the meantime, had also secured a local job as a result of her typing ability, and later went on to work as an educational welfare officer.

Their first mortgage in 1957 bought the couple a house in Eastwoodbury Lane, overlooking the airport. Graham remembers seeing the construction of an experimental aircraft, known as the Accountant. The house had apparently been used by the airport during the war as a billet for the air force, and cost £1,900, with repayments of £11 16s per week. Graham was rather proud of the fact that it was one of the first in the area to have brand-new replacement windows.

Life in the police force in the 1950s was community based, and Graham enjoyed the experience. Rules, back then, were often made to be broken. 'Uncle Bill' (PC, later Sergeant, Bill Gostling) on one occasion removed a rather lippy, disrespectful young man to rural Wakering and left him to walk back to Southend. The father of the lad complained about this treatment, but ended up giving his son a clip around the ear once 'Uncle' Bill had explained.

The retailers in Southend had a very good relationship with the police on their beat, and the police were looked after as a reward for their services. The fishmonger saved fresh fish (delivered overnight) for them, Offord's Bakery (near the current coach park) would supply freshly baked rolls, and Rossi's caretaker provided ice-cream if they turned up at a prescribed time during the night.

Graham learned to drive with the police force. Traffic sergeants were qualified examiners, and he passed his test in 1957. SMAC's (behind the old Odeon) would be willing to hire out vehicles to the police at a reasonable rate for a weekend – they were obviously regarded as a good risk.

After Graham started using a police scooter, one of the first uses of police radio communication was a call from a boat with a body on board. He drove along the Pier on his scooter to board the lifeboat, which took him to the boat concerned, and was persuaded to imbibe a tot of rum in true nautical fashion before dealing with the death, of natural causes. There was very little violence in the town, with an occasional affray at the Pier pavilion – during daytime dances! – which was attended by a blue police van, the Black Maria of its day.

A bit of a treat was being posted to 'cinema duty', a kindly act by the chief inspector on cold wet Sundays. Officers were instructed to stand at the back of one of the numerous cinemas in the town in the 1950s and they had access to many of the films of the day in this way, as long as they stayed in the spot allocated so that the chief knew where they were.

The police force had their own sports ground, in Wellstead Gardens, Westcliff, and here Graham played rugby for the police team. He also played snooker and darts, socially. The grounds were sold after the borough police disbanded, and the money went to the Police, Widows and Orphans Club.

The old police station in Alexandra Street and its ancillary buildings covered quite a bit of ground. The town's courts were behind the station itself, with the no. 1 court used as a crown court in the 1950s. Behind the courts were the bike sheds, bearing in mind the transport that most of the police were using then. There were also garages for police cars in Clarence Road, and stables for the police horses in Royal Mews. There was a club room that could accommodate police functions, but would be available at any time for snooker, perhaps bingo,

Southend-on-Sea Police rugby team, Priory Park, 1957. Back row, left to right: Kitch Lewis, Ted Lines, Bernard Broad, John Rodgers, John Griffin, John Bullivant, Terry Ford (captain), Dick Thatcher, John Cackett, Ray Chandler, Bill Kirley, Ernie Dark, the referee, Reg Evans. Front row: Eric Edwards, Graham Sargent, Brian Churcher, Dave Byrne, Eric Denney, Bert Williams. (Sargent collection)

raffles, and would be used for entertaining other visiting police forces. Later, there was a large purpose-built club room in Victoria Avenue, big enough for dances, and Graham was one of the DJs. At the back of the shops now in Alexandra Street was the mortuary, and over the top of the shops was the training room, the lecture room and the canteen. Because of Graham's catering experience, he often did the cooking here when on night duty.

Day shifts regularly saw him on the beat between Pier Hill and Victoria Circus. There were a couple of officers on one side of the railway bridge and a couple on the other, with an additional officer on Saturday when the High Street was extra busy with day trippers.

There was quite a bit of traffic duty, too, as there were far fewer traffic lights then, and as many as three officers could be on point duty at Victoria Circus at one time. In the summer, there were two PCs outside just about every pub at turn-out, lunchtime and evening, from the Kursaal to Pier Hill. Chinnery's seemed to attract the biggest crowds, but did not necessarily have any more trouble than anywhere else. There were also two PCs on horseback along Marine Parade, and two cars parked in Hartington Road – overall, a very prominent presence.

Local characters were much in evidence around the Southend High Street area. There was Sue, who sold the *Star* and the *Standard* outside the Odeon and was full of gossip, some of it very interesting to the police. Similarly, her brother Charlie, the paper-seller at Victoria Circus, was a fount of local knowledge. Graham knew all the bus drivers by name – one of them was married to a clippie who often passed on edible treats to the local bobbies. Within the force, one superintendent was known as the U-boat commander because he always wore a white silk scarf, making himself rather conspicuous at night.

Saturday nights during the illuminations were a particularly busy time for the local police. Although the coach park (Seaways) was much larger then, it was not big enough at this time of year. Convoys of coaches were lined up from Cuckoo Corner to Southend seafront, and a police motorcyclist would take them to one of the five coach parks near to the Kursaal (where Kursaal Estate is now) and along the seafront where the gasworks used to be. This was such a slow process that some coaches would be leaving, having seen the illuminations, as others were still queuing to get into the town.

The old blue police boxes then in evidence had flashing lights on top to indicate to the nearest officer that there was a message waiting. The idea was that you had to ensure you were at the boxes at specific times, and the box could be somewhere to eat your sandwiches, or to escape briefly from the cold or rain. But if you had the foresight to turn on the heater inside to warm up the box, the sergeant would turn it off unless you were actually in it. Another escape from bad weather was inside one of the City Bus Company's brown buses that were parked in Tylers Avenue, near the Regal Theatre. But you had to be careful you did not end up somewhere like Rayleigh if you fell asleep . . .

On the one hand, the police did not take themselves too seriously in the 1950s. They amused themselves by parking something on the hand or head of the Queen Victoria statue when she was at the top of Pier Hill (only if no one was looking of course), or even dropped non-dangerous debris such as an empty cigarette packet onto the heads of unsuspecting passers-by from their perch on top of the florist's near the railway bridge that crosses the High Street. On the other hand, however, they prided themselves on responding to 999 calls in just four minutes.

The white police helmets, associated with the borough police, distinguished them from other forces until 1969, when Southend amalgamated with Essex. These were tried out first by painting the dark helmets with white emulsion. As this passed muster, the force were issued not only with white helmets but with white gloves, and black gloves for night duty. Their raincoats and uniforms were made to measure by Horne Brothers, and became the envy of many other forces. There is apparently still a White Helmet Club, which meets annually at the 'new' Southend police station.

It was in 1961 that the old police station was moved to this modern structure, just off Victoria Avenue. Although Graham started to spend time here on training and recruiting, he was on duty during the Beatles' well-documented visit to the Odeon in Southend High Street in October 1963. He remembers them peeking out of their dressing-room windows overlooking Elmer Approach, which caused a surge of screaming females, but there were no real problems.

Graham was promoted to sergeant (yes, Sergeant Sargent) in 1966, and became more involved in training in matters of civil defence and new legislation, but the

The Borough Men marching past the old band-stage, Clifftown Parade, 1969. Graham is on the left in the front row, and a bemedalled Sergeant Bill Gostling is on the right of the front row. (Sargent collection)

Graham on duty when the Queen Mother, accompanied by the mayor, opened the Civic Centre, Victoria Avenue, 1967. (Sargent collection)

recruiting side of his work was made easy by the amount of officers who wanted to transfer to Southend, especially from London. One of the perks was considered to be the annual refund of tax that had been overpaid on the rent allowance, usually sufficient to pay for a holiday. A year later, he was on duty when the Queen Mother visited the town formally to open Southend's Civic Centre in Victoria Avenue in 1967, but he was not the sergeant who tripped and fell in front of her in the rush to be seen to be helpful.

During the 1960s, Graham and Shirley adopted two babies through two different agencies, one in London and one in Southend. Their son is Ian, and their daughter Jannette – spelt that way as a result of a spelling error in the adoption court.

Many years later, Graham is still involved with his local community, doing voluntary work at Southend Hospital.

Graham in his back garden with Jannette after his promotion, 1966. (Sargent collection)

DAVID SMITH

Dogs and Discs

At the beginning of the 1950s, David was a teenager at Eastwood High School. The area was then very rural, with a farm next door and a herd of cows. One of the teachers looked after the allotments, which were part of the school grounds, and part of the horticulture lessons. It was also possible to make money from the chickens kept on the grounds by paying 1s each for chicken-club shares, with the profits on egg sales distributed proportionately.

Looking back on schooldays, David's most abiding memory is perhaps his first sight of the head, Mr Taylor, in long black gown and mortar board: suitably impressive. But some of the teachers also made an impression: Mr Boyd threw a football at you if you were a nuisance, Miss Rose had a gift for acting out the parts of all the kings and queens being studied in the history class, and Mr Cooper (a later head) taught a geography class one day in which he posed the question 'Where is Aston Villa?' Obviously a football fan, he was not happy if you did not know the answer. Luckily for David, he was a football fan and still is. In fact, he was a member of the school football team.

Home was a rented terrace house in Rochester Drive, Westcliff. Apart from David, there was Mum, who worked for a while as a waitress at the Mount Liell Hotel overlooking Westcliff jetty, and Dad, originally a cellar man at the Carlton Hotel, Leigh-on-Sea, and then a porter at Southend General Hospital. The children in the Drive were a similar age, and their playground was the street, their cricket pitch being in the centre of the road. A car in the Drive was a novelty that drew admiring and curious attention. The house had a large garden, which meant that Dad could grow vegetables and keep chickens. Every year Dad bought a cockerel to fatten up for Christmas, but on one occasion the bird was particularly vicious, chasing David up the garden path in an attempt to grab a handful of his trousers and/or the flesh beneath. This was pretty scary for a youngster, and Dad decided that Christmas would come early that year.

David's grandma lived in Hainault Avenue in nearby Ashingdon. He was old enough to catch the no. 7 bus to Golden Cross on Sundays to visit her on his own because Mum and Dad often worked at weekends. He was fascinated by the wooden bungalow she lived in with its outside toilet. In the event of a long, hot summer, the overgrown grass alongside the railway lines at the bottom of the garden would become like a tinderbox, so when steam trains passed by, giving off sparks as they rumbled past, David would be ready with wet sacks to put out any fires that started. After Sunday lunch, he would make his way to

Sunday school at the St John Fisher Catholic Church at what is now known as Cuckoo Corner.

There was also a godmother who lived in an upstairs flat near the Grand Hotel, Leigh, who became friendly with a well-known local fishing family, the Osbornes. As a result of this friendship, David was able to experience a ride in a working cockle boat, and he remembers the smell, and the swell, with fondness. (Interestingly, there was also an aunt in London who was housekeeper for the actress Jean Kent in the late 1940s, and early 1950s, which secured David some 'odd jobs' at the London Palladium.)

He left school in 1952, aged 15, and studied civil engineering for a year at the Municipal College, then at Victoria Circus. Although he thought this might suit him as it combined his interest in maths and drawing, it was not as attractive a proposition as he had envisaged. Dad thought it would be a good idea for him to work in the printing trade, and, although David had reservations, he started working at Richmond Art, a small printer's in Richmond Avenue, Westcliff, that specialised in photo albums. He was working here during the 1953 floods, and went over to Canvey Island to help a co-worker whose mother-in-law had been drowned when their bungalow was flooded. As for the job, David felt he was more of a dogsbody than a printer so he moved on to Thamesmouth Printing Press, another local employer, at a wage of £4 17s per week with overtime on Saturdays. Such an option was not for him if Southend United were playing at home.

Incidentally, if Southend were playing away, local fans often utilised the John Smith Coach Company, which seemed to operate with one rusty coach and which often did not make it home – whether because of the coach or the driver is debatable – meaning that the occupants slept in the coach overnight. But it was cheap.

As far as David's career was concerned, he did not think there seemed much point in following a printing apprenticeship as such, given that National Service was approaching, but he stayed with Thamesmouth until 1955. While there he made some lasting friends among the twenty or thirty staff in the compositing and machining rooms, and this camaraderie was one of the best parts of the job. On a day-to-day basis, he was feeding paper through large industrial machinery, which printed labels for Glaxo Pharmaceuticals (their main client) and red and silver cigarette packets for Philip Morris. He was not allowed near the typesetting, which would have seen him having union problems (NATSOPA). The ladies there were restricted to finishing, folding, cutting and, inevitably, teamaking.

When the annual dinner-dance came around, David encouraged his friend Lawrie to take ballroom-dancing lessons at Mimi Green's in London Road. Although Lawrie started off with two left feet, the lessons worked, even though they had to learn to dance with a chair instead of a partner, and in spite of the sight of a hysterical window cleaner observing at least one of these lessons.

By the 1950s David's dad had become involved in organising social events and whist drives for staff and patients at Southend Hospital. Perhaps the most dramatic were the annual Guy Fawkes firework displays and bonfires painstakingly set up in a grassed area of the hospital grounds. This took place in full view, but at a safe distance, of the children's ward, and some of the young patients could come out onto balconies for a closer look. Every year, Keddies, the department store in Southend High Street, generously provided a broken or otherwise redundant dummy which could be dressed up as the Guy atop the bonfire. Initially, these dummies were allowed to collapse into the fire once the flames took hold, but this rather spoiled the effect, so one year David's dad decided to rig up a rather elaborate suspension system so that the dummy would remain as a focus for longer. What he had forgotten was that the clothes would burn away quickly, leaving the sight of a dangling naked body exposed to a lot of giggling children. The suspension idea was not repeated.

At the end of the working day, David was not averse to earning extra money, and this rather replaced a social life. He worked as a runner for the bookmaker at the greyhound stadium in Sutton Road, collecting some generous tips. There was an instance of a dog-owner putting a lot of money on his own dog and losing – so he paid the bookmaker with the dog. The bookmaker told David to take it home and look after it, so David put the dog in their empty coal shed, but the greyhound's barking during the night set off the six dachshunds inside the house (he was not the only dog lover in the family). As a result, at six o'clock the next morning he removed the hapless dog, and tied it to the knocker of the bookmaker's door. There was another incident when a new, untrained dog got knocked over at the first bend of a race and decided to take a short cut over the middle of the track, causing the race to be abandoned.

Another way of spending Friday evenings was by playing records at a variety of dance venues. These included the Studio, then at Chalkwell Park, Alan Mitchell's above the Civic Cinema at Victoria Circus, Mimi Green's, and the Stansted Club in London Road, then run by a 'professor' and complete with glitter ball but now a synagogue. The venues provided the records, with music from ballroom through Dickie Valentine to Bill Haley, although the latter took some time to gain popularity it seems, even among the young. David's role was then called the steward, not the disc jockey. There was no pay, just free entry – and the pure pleasure of it. These venues were all very similar as far as David was concerned, as were

RITZ :: Southend-on-Sea
Telephone 66683
General Manager   .·.   .·.   .·.   .·.   .·.   .·.   G. A. NIMSE

SUNDAY, 6th JUNE, 1954

Jack Parnell

Programme ⸱ ⸱ 6d.

Ritz programme, 1954. (Smith collection)

Palace Theatre programme, 1955, featuring the young Ronald Barker as Hercule Poirot in Alibi. *(Smith collection)*

PALACE THEATRE
WESTCLIFF

**Evening 8.0
27 Aug. '55**

G. Circle 4/6
Including Tax

H 14

TO BE RETAINED

WILLIAM HEAVEN

presents

"ALIBI"
By AGATHA CHRISTIE

CHARACTERS IN THE ORDER OF THEIR APPEARANCE :

Mrs. Ackroyd	GWEN LEWIS
Flora Ackroyd	EDNA HOPCROFT
Major Blunt	REGINALD JESSUP
Parker	LIONEL GADSDEN
Ursula Bourne	MARGARET BROGAN
Geoffrey Raymond	ARNOLD YARROW
Caryl Sheppard	JANETTE GARRARD
Hercule Poirot	RONALD BARKER
Doctor Sheppard	IAN AINSLEY
Inspector Davies	HENRY RAYNER
Sir Roger Ackroyd	EDWIN MORTON
Ralph Paton	PETER WHITBREAD

The Play Directed By ROGER WILLIAMS

SYNOPSIS OF SCENES :

ACT I   The hall at Sir Roger Ackroyd's, Fernly Park.

Scene I   Afternoon.
Scene II   After Dinner.

ACT II   The next morning.

ACT III   Scene I   Four days later.
Scene II   The next night.

Company Manager
Stage Manager .... HAYDN DAVIES
.... CLAIRE LA FONTAINE

Scenery by Stage Productions Co   Furniture by Old Times Furnishing Co., Ltd.
Lighting by Strand Electric   Props by Prop Shop and Stage Properties Ltd.
Flowers by Floreat.

For PALACE THEATRE

Licensee and General Manager ....
Theatre Manager .... HERBERT J. POINTER, F.I.M.E.M.
.... WILLIAM T. TATE, A.I.M.E.M.

In accordance with the requirements of the Watch Committee :— (a) The Public may leave at the end of the performance by all exits and entrances and the doors of such exits and entrances shall at that time be open. (b) All gangways, passages and staircases shall be kept entirely free from chairs or any other obstructions. (c) Persons shall not be permitted to stand or sit in any of the intersecting gangways. If standing be permitted at the rear of the seating, sufficient space shall be left for persons to pass easily to and fro. (d) The fireproof curtain shall at all times be maintained in working order and shall be lowered during the interval time of every performance

The Management reserve the right to refuse admission also to make any alteration in the cast which may be rendered necessary by illness or other unavoidable causes.

REFRESHMENTS

Refreshments are served in the auditorium during intervals—please order in advance from the attendant who seats you. Coffee, sandwiches, soft drinks, etc. can be obtained from the Kiosk in the Foyer.
THE TAKING OF PHOTOGRAPHS IN THE THEATRE IS FORBIDDEN.

their customers. The girls in A-line skirts, some sporting 'bubble' haircuts, boys in brothel creepers (because of their thick, quiet soles), drainpipe trousers and velvet jackets.

David did find time for the occasional dance on Saturday night at the Kursaal, and he was a fan of the big bands that appeared on a Friday night if he was not working. When there was an (unusual) show of fisticuffs on the dance floor one evening, he remembers Johnny Dankworth playing 'God Save the Queen' on his saxophone as a couple of policemen frogmarched off the culprits. There were live bands on Sundays at the Golden Lion, the Spread Eagle, the Blue Boar (all local pubs) and at the Ritz. It was interesting to see that David had watched the young, emerging Ronald Barker playing Poirot at the Palace Theatre, Westcliff, in 1955, naturally unaware of the significance the young actor would later have in very different roles.

After National Service (with just one night spent overseas – in Cyprus – for no apparent reason), he worked with EKCO on their production line at the Kenway branch in Southend, making what would now be regarded as rather large transistor radios. When redundancies hit in the 1950s, EKCO showed themselves to be caring employers by bringing in a selection of personnel staff to interview people in situ to help them secure another job as quickly as possible. As a result, David worked for BATA shoes at Tilbury, but unfortunately only for a couple of days – the assembly line that produced wellington boots was not for him. He certainly settled down in his next job with Ford's at Dagenham, because he was with them for the next thirty years.

Although David's days of stewarding were no longer possible, given his new working hours, he did not miss out on his music. He had a Pye Black Box record player, and spent money in Gilbert's, Southchurch Road, on such records as Bill Haley and Lonnie Donegan. These he played in the one unused room at home – it came into its own only on Sundays and special occasions – but even so it was not as far removed from his dad as the latter would have liked.

David actually saw the Beatles twice at the Odeon in Southend High Street in 1963. Their first visit in May was uneventful, at a time when they were relegated to fourth billing, with Roy Orbison at the top. The second visit in October was a very different story following their success with 'Please Please Me' and 'She Loves You'. This time he had to sleep on the pavement to get tickets, and on the day he heard very little of the concert but was memorably showered with jelly babies intended for George Harrison.

On one of his intermittent visits to the Kursaal, he met his first wife. They married in 1960, but divorced not many years later after their two daughters were born, and after living in at least five different places in and around Southend. Subsequently, David met Gloria in the Harrows, now the Dick Turpin, on the A127. She was 19, a Londoner living in Benfleet, and working for her dad who had a profitable business selling hair lacquers and shampoos. This particular evening, Dad was late meeting her for an end-of-day sales update, so Gloria, with some trepidation, went to look for him in the bar. Who should she meet instead but David and his friend Desmond. David, although perhaps just a little impressed with Gloria's confidence (and with her Austin Metropolitan soft-top with its

David Smith and Gloria after their wedding in 1966 at Southend register office in the new Civic Centre building, Victoria Avenue. (Smith collection)

Double christening with Gloria and Stuart on the left, and Julia with Michael on the right. (Smith collection)

Fraser Nash engine!), ended up a little the worse for wear, and it was Gloria who took *him* home. They arranged a date, and married three years later in 1966.

The wedding ring was bought at the jeweller's in Talza Arcade (now Victoria Circus), which sported a mysterious sign announcing: 'I will pierce your ears while you wait.' The wedding itself was arranged at short notice with a special licence at the register office in the Civic Centre, Victoria Avenue. They had just 7s 6d left after the wedding until David's next payday, partly thanks to having to pay not just rent in advance for their first home together, but also key money. Married life kicked off in a dark flat in Westborough Road, Westcliff, at the top of a flight of long, narrow stairs, although they did at least have their own front door.

Their son, Stuart, was born the same year. Their next son, Harvey, was born in 1968, but Graham was a 1970s baby. All the boys were born at home. Stuart's christening at Hanningfield, near Wickford, was a bit of an occasion. He was christened at the same time as Gloria's new nephew, Michael. Gloria's sister, Julia, had given birth to Michael just eleven weeks after Stuart had been born, but after many years of trying for a baby. The vicar (name of Middleton) who christened the boys had married Gloria's parents in east London, and had christened Gloria.

JOHN HART

Not Always Bleak

B orn in Rochford Hospital, John has lived in Southend-on-Sea all his life. His dad was originally a master baker who had to retire from the work because of dermatitis. His mum was a housewife, and he has an older brother, Alfred, who emigrated to New Zealand in the late 1950s. When he was growing up, the family lived in Moseley Street, Southend. A neighbour was a friend of Petula Clark, who often visited.

He used to walk to school in Hamstel Road, picking blackberries on the way. By 1950, he was at Southchurch Hall School, now Ambleside College, where boys and girls were segregated. The school even instituted different times for the boys and girls to finish their school day, in an effort to keep them apart, but this does not seem to have worked.

The uniform was dark blue with a shell badge on the jacket, and merit marks were awarded for wearing full uniform, which John acquired as and when his family could afford to buy each separate piece. (His dad was now working for the Co-op in Southchurch Road as a handyman.) Merit marks were also awarded – by Mr Johns, if he remembers rightly – to the naughty as a bribe for being good, which seemed, and still seems, grossly unfair to John. More fair perhaps was Mr Carlisle's idea of getting guilty culprits to choose their own punishment.

He did not stay to school dinner, but often went to Price's Bakery en route and bought a 1*d* 'Nelson Slab', filling and hot. Food at home was often a result of self-sufficiency as John's mum kept chickens for eggs and for eating, and rabbits. Even the one rabbit that had been kept as a family pet was cooked and eaten one day, much to the boys' disgust. Their cat, Pete, managed to keep away from the poultry but liked to sit atop a high fence and swat the feathers that were then a popular trim for ladies' hats.

At home, the radio played an important part in family life. Billy Cotton's *Wakey Wakey* was particularly popular on Sundays. Weekends were often spent visiting relatives. John's granddad lived in Brays Lane, Rochford, and had a large garden and orchard where the family could help themselves to plums and other fruit. Holidays were often also a case of descending on relatives – there were family members in Kent. But the annual Southend carnival became rather a feature, as did paddle-steamer trips from the end of the Pier in the 1950s and 1960s to places like Margate.

There was also the wind-up record player. One unforgettable purchase in John's early record collection was called 'The Flies Crawled up the Window' – or so he claims. He used to win bets if someone denied its existence.

Thorpe Bay beach, at the bottom of Lifstan Way, c. 1950. Left to right: cousin Sandra Goudie, destined to become a BEA cover girl as an air hostess, cousin Sheila Goudie, John Hart, Aunt Hetty Marchant and David Watkins, next-door neighbour. (Hart collection)

The only sport John particularly enjoyed as a child was fishing, but rather than the salt-water areas around Southend, he and his brother favoured the Little Baddow area, farther north. He still has his split-cane rod. He did become a member of the school cricket team, however, and they played at the gasworks grounds, adjoining Eton House private school.

In Southend, John became the no. 1 member of the Gaumont Saturday Morning Picture Club, and has fond memories of the many cinemas in the town at the time. As well as the films, he remembers seeing variety at the Regal, repertory at the Plaza (Stratford Johns appeared there at one point), and Louis Armstrong – complete with spotted handkerchief – at the Odeon, probably in the 1960s.

In 1953 John left school, aged 15. This was also the year of the coronation – with a street party in Moseley Street – and of the local floods. He recalls that there was no entry into Southchurch Park as a result, and that his aunt who lived in nearby Shaftesbury Avenue had to contend with water 5ft deep.

His first job was in Trinity Road, Southend, in a small factory that made musical boxes. Then he spent a couple of years making spectacle frames for a company called Merx in Aneley Road, Westcliff, where he worked with Howard Baker's singer (a popular local band). Eventually, John started an apprenticeship as an electrician with Frost and Co. in Princes Street, Southend, for 11¾d per hour. Only when he joined the union did his wages begin to increase. This apprenticeship lasted for four years and served him well, because he went on to work in oil refineries and power stations once he had qualified.

Howard Baker and his Broadcasting Band, mid-1950s. (Smeeton collection)

One particular job in the 1960s took him to Thorpe Bay, where he spotted someone acting oddly in the long grass as he pushed his bicycle across the railway line. Only when he saw the local paper the next day did he realise he had seen Ronnie Biggs, of Great Train Robbery fame, on the run.

In the evenings, a favourite venue was the Castle pub on Southend seafront, which featured a jazz band upstairs, including the likes of Terry Lightfoot. Across the road from the Castle was a café that also had a live group. Tuesday evenings were spent at the Anchor at Wakering, and there was, again, a café nearby which was open late for coffees. There were a few attempts at learning to dance at Victor Sylvester's dance studio above the Odeon in the High Street, but John admits that this was never his strong point.

For transport, John had a Bond mini-car motorbike with three wheels that had to be kickstarted, and then a Reliant Regal. At the age of 20, John got his first motorbike, a Frances Barnett, known as a Fanny B, at a time when helmets were not necessary for him or whichever girl might be on the back. He passed his driving test at the fourth attempt, when he finally received a compliment, as being the best 'steerer' the examiner had ever come across, no doubt as a result of his experience driving a three-wheeler.

In his spare time, John enjoyed playing cricket and football. He was the secretary for the Bleak Lodge cricket team at Victory Sports Ground for six years, and played as fielder and spin bowler. Their name was apparently acquired from the place they used to meet up – an old dilapidated building called Bleak Lodge at

John as a member of Bleak Lodge Cricket Club, at the rear of the Moseley Street house, c. 1960. (Hart collection)

the back of the Halfway House pub in Thorpe Bay. He played football for the electricity board (Estric), and for Earls Hall United and Shoebury Town – and scored the winning goal in his last game for the latter before committing more time to work and to his new family.

One of John's friends had a sister living in Liverpool who visited the family for a holiday, and this sister – Jessica – was to become John's wife in 1965. The wedding was at All Saints on the corner of Sutton Road, and the reception was at Garons in Hamlet Court Road. The wedding photographs, according to the photographer, had not developed because of a camera problem, although John found out much later that this was not quite true: in fact, the quality was so poor that the photographer could not confess to his inadequacy.

For their first year as a married couple, Jessica found work in a shoe shop in Hamlet Court Road, and they lived in the top part of a house, which involved sharing a bathroom with the landlord. However, only a year later, John managed to find a run-down house in The Grove, Southend, which had been home to rather a lot of cats. Undeterred, the couple secured a mortgage of £17 per month to pay off the asking price of £2,350. Their son, David, was born in Rochford Hospital in 1967, and John is still at that very same address, although the marriage, sadly, lasted little more than a decade.

David's first pram was second-hand and broken, and John spent some time riveting and painting it until it looked the part. The couple also invested in a twin-tub washing machine, and John's parents were willing babysitters when the need arose, so they managed quite well.

By the late 1960s, John was the proud owner of a cine-camera, and he had also acquired a guitar along the way from the music shop near the Bluebird Café in Southend. But, like his penchant for poetry at school, such pursuits were short-lived. Unlike his interest in Southend-on-Sea.

BRIAN SMEETON

Ducking and Diving

Brian has spent all his life in Southend. He was born in Rochford Hospital before the war, and he and his five sisters and three brothers were brought up in a two-bedroom rented house in Station Avenue, off East Street, until 1951. His dad cycled miles for work wherever he could find it after leaving the Army, mainly on building sites.

Schooling was at St Mary's, Prittlewell, and then Wentworth High School for Boys in Wentworth Road. Playgrounds included the Black Pit, the local name for the dredged sand pit that subsequently became Roots Hall. Brian and his friends enjoyed waiting for the trays of meat pies from Telfords Bakery near Roots Hall to be put out to cool on large trolleys – rather convenient for little hands. He was once caught bunking off school to see Tommy Lawton play for Notts County. He managed to get himself stuck on the barbed wire and was rescued by a policeman, but, luckily for him, the PC saw him safely inside the stadium.

An early Saturday job was as delivery boy for Garons bakers (they had a factory at the back of the current police station off Victoria Avenue), and then there was his milk round for Howard's Dairies about 1950, which paid *2s 6d* a day on Saturdays and Sundays. Deliveries were around the Westcliff-on-Sea area, and after being paid Brian would walk to the Grainger Close entrance of the football stadium (then in Sutton Road) where he could sneak in under the turnstile for free. After a game, there was often discarded booty to be found on the floor.

He also collected scrap paper for Holland's, the waste-paper merchants in Prince Avenue, and was doing just this one day when he and a friend heard a loud aircraft noise and the very loud sound of a crash. They walked all the way to Bournemouth Park Road, several miles away, to find the source of what had obviously been an aircraft crash, and had the dubious pleasure of seeing the small plane spreadeagled up a tree, through a roof, and partly in an adjoining alley. The injured pilot had already been removed before they got there.

In the early 1950s, the family moved to a much larger house in Hamlet Court Road, with a bathroom, four bedrooms and even a peach tree in the garden. Brian's mum raised chickens to sell on in this garden, and he remembers the day six of the (white) chickens disappeared and his mum not only accused the local butcher but made sure she got the plucked and trussed birds back! He also talks about the rubber spectacles that she made for one of the chickens who kept pecking the others – there was no glass in them, but the built-up sides acted in a similar way to blinkers so that the chicken could not see her victims so readily.

Brian Smeeton's early home in Hamlet Court Road, mid-1950s. (Smeeton collection)

Brian left school in 1953, and he and his friends were big fans of the cinema in that decade, spoiled as they were by the prolific choice in the Southend area, from the Mascot to the Coliseum, the Metropole, and Garons (1*s* to sit anywhere) among others. It was not unusual for a group of them to go to see a different film on three or four consecutive nights. He usually paid, of course, though remembers one occasion sneaking in to see Jane Russell in *The Outlaw* at the Civic News Theatre in Talza Arcade, which brought discovery and instant expulsion – though this was probably pre-1950, given the film's release date. The owner of the Strand Cinema had an effective way of dealing with undesirables, it seems. First, he ensured there were two queues, one for the respectable, the second for the less so, and he would check these queues at intervals himself (especially the second) and turf out anyone he did not like the look of. Live acts were also available at the local cinemas. In the 1950s, Brian saw Stan Kenton ('too loud') and Winifred Atwell at the Odeon in Southend High Street.

Apart from the cinemas, other live acts were in abundance, including variety shows on the Pier, featuring such local luminaries as Peggy Mount. There was live music at the Palace Hotel featuring the Paramounts in the 1960s (later the roots of Procul Harum). There was also the London Hotel on the corner of the High Street (where Clinton Cards is now) featuring the Barracudas with their unusual two-armed guitar, the Ranch House opposite Priory Park gates which had a 'real' tree growing out of the middle of the dance floor, and the Elms in London Road.

One place where the music emanated just as often from a record player as from a live band was Mimi Green's on Saturday nights. This was a ballroom (upstairs) with a little restaurant downstairs, in London Road – it is still a dance studio. Mimi's husband Morris was the doorman, although it seems he disappeared at the first sign of trouble. The heavily made-up Mimi liked to pair couples off if she saw any wallflowers, without being subtle about it – for instance: 'She's dying for a dance.'

At the Kursaal, Brian saw Eric Delaney and, of course, Tornado Smith. The Kursaal issued green cards, which gave preferential rates to local residents. These were really useful, and Brian favoured the snooker room and the water chute, though he also saw such sideshows as the stuffed whale, Al Capone's car and the talking head. He also remembers Happy Harry preaching along the seafront, drawing custom away from the Salvation Army nearby. Perversely, however, some people thought it amusing to heat up coins with a cigarette lighter before passing them over (ouch). Happy Harry's signature tune, if Brian remembers rightly, was:

It's rolling in, it's rolling in,
The Sea of Love is rolling in.
And I believe, and I receive
The Sea of Love – it's rolling in.

Passers-by also gave money to the chap who drew pictures in the sand near to the Pier, and at an old mariner and 'loveable scrounger' who could whirl his pipe like no other, known, predictably, as Popeye.

As to employment, Brian's first job was with Carter Paterson, the national express carriers, assisting with local deliveries in their old green lorries. He hung on the back on a chain, standing on the tailboard, and travelled at around 30mph for £1 5s per week. He feels that being a good goalkeeper helped him stabilise the stacks of boxes crammed into these vehicles.

Then he worked on the dodgems at the Olympia, which subsequently featured wrestling and dancing. This venue was at the bottom of Pier Hill, run by Mr and Mrs Desmond, who paid him £3 5s per week. Each of the three lads had five cars

to look after, and often picked up 'tips' in the form of coins left lying around, often having been bounced out of pockets. This job was seven days a week until 10 p.m., but Brian enjoyed jumping on and off the cars to collect the fares, and never had an accident. During this period, he remembers visits from the American Navy on the USS *Shea* and the USS *Gyatt*, which caused a few minor skirmishes, but they were big spenders to compensate. The Swedish Navy also put in an appearance and they were much more amenable.

He then worked for the drinks company Corona, delivering as far as Tilbury from its base in Vale Avenue, off Sutton Road. Most of the customers were retail outlets, but there were also householders who bought 6d savings stamps for Christmas and returned used bottles for a few pence.

The dodgems below the Olympia Ballroom, Pier Hill, c. 1955. Brian is on the left. (Smeeton collection)

Left to right: Derek Witridge, Sven ?, Brian, Terry Bell (?) with Johnny Holliday kneeling, at the Pop Inn, c. 1957. (Smeeton collection)

All the bottles then were glass, with metal flick tops, and all the drinks were soft drinks, such as dandelion and burdock. Brian was involved in the loading onto open-back lorries, and sat by the driver, working six days a week, with overtime at Christmas. The most complicated part of the job was sorting out the money, dividing it between sales, stamps, returns – and not forgetting tips.

This was when he started learning to drive. It was also when he developed an interest in Italian suits, drainpipe trousers, multicoloured hooped socks and narrow ties. The suits were made by Lipscombe's in Queen's Road – they sent someone home to measure up, and then the suit could be paid for in instalments. To get the right look for his hair, there was George's in Sutton Road or Costa's in Queen's Road. A fond memory is of cruising the seafront in his friend Johnny Holliday's pink Standard Eight convertible coupé featuring windscreen washers that could be operated in a way that drenched the pedestrians. This was a great attraction for the local girls, although it eventually fell apart – literally.

Brian and Julie at the Elms, London Road, Leigh, 1963. (Smeeton collection)

Of course these kind of diversions were drastically interrupted by National Service. Brian was a regimental signaller with the Royal Artillery from 1957 to 1959, spending twenty months in Cyprus. He and his peers met up during leave from National Service in places such as the Goldmine in Southchurch Road near Victoria Circus, a coffee bar/café with a jukebox, or the Pop Inn at Station Road, Westcliff, which also had a dance floor. Victoria Circus was also the location for what were known as the 'suicide toilets' because they were right in the centre so that you had to dodge trolley buses and cars to reach them.

In the 1960s, Brian worked mainly on building sites, and his musical taste veered towards trad jazz. The Pier had live jazz, as did the Elms, and Brian saw Clinton Ford, Kenny Ball and Acker Bilk locally. It was at the Elms that he met Julie, from Wickford, in 1963. Julie originally commuted to London to work but then found a job as a Dictaphone typist nearer home with Willis Faber & Dumas, close to the Cliffs Pavilion. It was also at the Elms that he recalls seeing Helen Mirren, a local resident, before she went on to fame and fortune.

Brian remembers proposing at the Odeon, and he married Julie in 1965 at St Catherine's in Wickford, with a reception at the Castle in the town. His father-in-law gave him his first car, a second-hand Consul Mark I. His first driving test started off badly because he left his glasses in the car, so could not read the number plate as requested before getting into the vehicle. The second was more successful, and he passed comfortably. He managed to run the car on £1 per week.

The first married home was a flat in Ambleside Drive. Brian and Julie's first daughter, Paula, was born in 1966, and they had two other girls, the third born when they had secured a two-bedroom council house in Lincoln Chase a few years later. Nowadays they live in a bungalow in a peaceful part of Southchurch.

JOHN COPPINS

Steam and Ships

Although John was born in Great Wakering just before the war, his family moved to Fernbrook Avenue, Southchurch, in 1944 and he lived there until 1977. The move was a result of his father's desire to be nearer to his job at the Kursaal. Dad was the foreman of the then-extensive Kursaal grounds, involved principally in their maintenance. The reduced commute was much easier on him and his bicycle.

John's early memories of living in Southend in the 1950s are of the Elim Pentecostal Church in Seaview Road. The Sunday-school services were particularly impressive with their abundance of evangelical singing and music, and the enthusiastic commitment of the Irish pastor. It was at this very church that his older sister, Dolly, met and married her husband, a chef, although the couple moved to London.

At the start of the 1950s John was still at primary school, Thorpe School in Lifstan Way. This was then a very rural area made up of cornfields and farmland. Nature study classes at school served to emphasise for the children this proximity of nature. A highlight of primary school was the annual teachers-versus-pupils cricket match in the school playing fields, with Mr Spurling being particularly skilled, and Mrs Riley obscuring the wicket with her ample proportions. A downside was the occasional asthma attack that bothered John as a boy. A consequence of the latter was that he was well known to his local GP, one of the few people who John knew with a car. This resulted in John being offered a lift one day on his way to school: his first trip in a motor car and quite an occasion.

Close to his home, he could see the steam trains rumbling over the bridge, and there were banks between the houses and the bridge where he and his friends could play freely. This started him on a lifelong love of trains and railways, which was obviously a family trait in that his influential maternal grandfather was a railwayman from 1895 until his retirement in 1944.

Other youthful occupations were regular visits to the beach, which was within walking distance, although Mum insisted that he kept his sandals on while paddling. While on the beach, John could watch the grab cranes lifting coal from the collier ships moored at the gasworks' jetty and depositing them onto the conveyor belt that moved the coal to its resting place on the shore. He also seems to have rather enjoyed the sight of the trolley-bus conductor grappling with the pole underneath the bus to try and manoeuvre the pantograph (the link between

Steam train at Southend Central station, mid-1950s. (Peter Ashton collection)

the trolley bus and the overhead wires) back into position on the occasions when it came off the wire and fell onto the roof.

His local cinema was the Plaza, and John enjoyed the cowboy films, as did his mother. John was also happy to accompany his mum when she went shopping, and felt useful by helping her carry the heavy bags. The nearest grocer's was Mead's opposite the Salvation Army hall, which cut ham to order and filled customers' bags from their shopping lists. There were also regular visits to the Talza Arcade at the top of the High Street, where John's favourite shop seems to have been Bobin's, the bookshop, a family concern, where he could buy comics such as the *Beano*, *Dandy*, *Hotspur* and *Rover*, for around 1*d* apiece.

Less frequent was the carnival, an annual treat. The carnival queens were generally quite a bit older then than in the twenty-first century. John's dad knew the driver of the Kursaal Flyer so that made it doubly interesting for John, who also felt that the floats from the local theatre clubs were usually outstanding.

His interest in trains developed during his time at secondary school, Shoebury High. On Saturday afternoons he would watch the ins and outs of the engines at the terminal at the side of the Civic Centre in Victoria Avenue. This area was largely devoted to allotments at the time. In the early 1950s, John acquired a box Brownie to take photographs of these engines, but it soon became clear this was not efficient enough for his needs, so he progressed by the mid-1950s to a Brownie Cresta with a much clearer viewfinder. Soon after, the steam service came to an end at Southend Victoria station. Luckily for him, his technology teacher at Shoebury High must have had similar interests, because in 1955 he took the whole class on a trip to Swindon Railway Works where they could see at close hand the boilers, the riveting and the molten metal.

Shoebury High had not been the obvious choice academically, but John did not want to learn Latin, which was on offer at other, and nearer, schools. He was

The Talza Arcade, as it was known, Victoria Circus, mid-1950s. (Nicholls collection)

happy to undertake the 3-mile journey to school on the bus every day, a rural trip where he could spot hares and rabbits en route. However, Mr Napier, the head, was a bit terrifying in his cap and gown. He was known as Snapper, and believed in the cane as a form of retribution. On the one occasion that John was summoned to his presence after talking in assembly, Snapper was called away, so he escaped the caning experience. John could have got into the head's good books if he had been less nervous about his singing, because this was seemingly one of Mr Napier's passions. The school song was Elgar's 'Pomp and Circumstance no. 4: All Men Must be Free', and this had to be sung on all special occasions. A new head, Mr Mills, was appointed in the mid-1950s, and he changed the school song, which John felt was a great pity.

Mr Randall was another teacher who made an impression on John. He taught English and religious education and managed to find enough humour in the Bible to keep the boys' attention. This teacher wrote poems for the school magazine, *The Tideway*, and also shone at the annual tennis match between pupils and teachers. PE was a bit of a trial for John, as his asthma was restrictive, although he was provided with an inhaler eventually. He did join the rest of his class at the open-air swimming pool on Westcliff seafront on Wednesday afternoons, but never did learn to swim. The PE teacher was known as Spring, a popular public school name for PE teachers apparently.

The Shoebury uniform was a black blazer with a red and black striped tie, available from Meakers, the uniform shop in Southend High Street. The school houses were Nore, Cambridge, Maplin and Ness, all suitably nautical.

Because Dad worked at the Kursaal, John was able to use some of its facilities free of charge, and he made the most of the opportunity. Dad worked at the weekends and John would incorporate a visit to see him with a ride on his favourite, the water chute, especially before it was 'tamed' by being confined to a fixed rail. He also liked taking the boat through the illuminated caves, the miniature railway that was a feature in the early 1950s, and the carousels, which were then known as gallopers, because of the prevalence of prancing horses. John recalls that the Wall of Death rider, Tornado Smith, used to ride a penny-farthing bicycle around Southend to publicise his act.

The coronation and the Canvey floods, both in 1953, figure equally in John's memories – the coronation because the street party was rained off and everyone decamped to the nearby, happy-to-oblige, garage next to the Salvation Army hall, and the floods because he stood on Pier Hill, looking down at Peter Pan's playground, which had effectively become part of the estuary apart from the tops of the helter-skelter and the crazy house, the only parts visible above the water. Incidentally, in the 1950s, the street lights were not on all night in the town, but, presumably because there were fewer cars, this did not seem to cause any problems.

In 1955, John left school. His first job was with Proberts, a printer's in Southchurch Road. He had thought that bookbinding might suit him as he was interested in books, but it was not quite what he had expected. Soon after, he joined the town's biggest employer, E.K. Cole. He started as an office boy in the Plastics Division, working for Mr Radford's secretary. As a junior, he got to know everyone when wandering around, becoming fond of the scientific director's secretary, known as Auntie. EKCO was for John a very happy place to work, although he seems to have spent the first six months making cups of tea.

Progress was reasonably swift, however. First junior clerk and then sales order clerk, within the Shipping and Export Division. He worked mainly with young men like himself, although there was one ex-Wren who swore more than they did. At Christmas time, the Shipping Division treated themselves to an appropriate tot of rum in their tea to celebrate. Interdepartmental sporting contests were a regular feature of life at EKCO: darts, bowls, even table football. Was the bought ledger department perhaps the most competitive? Maybe.

The Shipping Division dealt with just about every country in the world, including such as India, New Zealand and Columbia. It was quite a regular occurrence for a foreign delegation to visit EKCO, and then the gold EKCO flag was replaced with the appropriate national flag. When a Russian delegation visited in the 1950s, the union made a formal objection to the flying of their flag as there was still a lot of anti-communist feeling around. A nearby building hoisted the Union Jack at this point, making its own silent protest perhaps.

In his spare time, John's interest in railways continued apace. The year 1956 was the 100th anniversary of the railway coming to Southend. John visited a temporary exhibition upstairs at the Odeon in the High Street with a whole host of memorabilia, and where British Rail had provided a mock-up cab of their express engine, the Britannia, which visitors could pretend to drive. A special train was laid on to Fenchurch Street, with a London, Tilbury and Southend Railway coach featuring people in Victorian clothes, although unfortunately the day also featured some heavy downpours. This train, beautifully restored, did a couple of rail tours, and its engine (the Thundersley) is preserved at Bressingham, near Diss in Norfolk.

John's dad had been in the Auxiliary Fire Service during the Second World War, and John inherited a more unusual interest – in fires. When he got off the bus in 1959 and saw the smoke billowing at the shore end of the Pier, he could not resist having a closer look. He followed the smoke to where the fire was raging that demolished the Pier pavilion ballroom. Back-up had already arrived for the Southend brigade from outlying areas, but they seemed less hands-on than the

Railway centenary celebrations programme,
1956. (Smeeton collection)

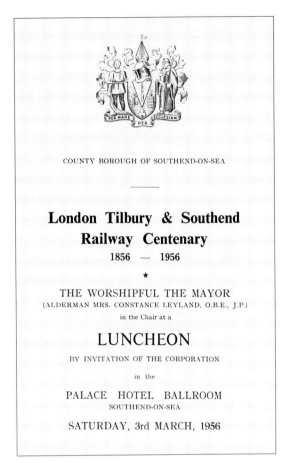

COUNTY BOROUGH OF SOUTHEND-ON-SEA

———

London Tilbury & Southend
Railway Centenary
1856 — 1956

★

THE WORSHIPFUL THE MAYOR
(ALDERMAN MRS. CONSTANCE LEYLAND, O.B.E., J.P.)

in the Chair at a

LUNCHEON

BY INVITATION OF THE CORPORATION

in the

PALACE HOTEL BALLROOM
SOUTHEND-ON-SEA

SATURDAY, 3rd MARCH, 1956

Southend teams, although this is only John's opinion. He also seems to have been on hand at the time of the subsequent fires on the Pier.

The South Essex Railway Society were advertising for members in Mac's Hobby Store in Talza Arcade in 1962, and John decided to join. This was the year that the last steam business train from Fenchurch Street to Thorpe Bay was specially preened and polished for its final trip. John was on this train, the 6.12 service, which was full of people with the same interest, and the business commuters had the opportunity to say their goodbyes to the crew, many of whom left the railways afterwards. Special announcements were made en route, but John still felt that there was a lack of appropriate ceremony. This train, the 42501, finally left Shoeburyness in February 1963, its light engine broken up in Derby, which seems a sad, rather unrecognised, farewell.

Although John's main interest in the 1960s was in attending railway lectures and talks, and visiting railway installations, he also acquired a taste for folk music, perhaps inherited from his grandfather, who enjoyed entertaining people with his singing. He heard the original Seekers but was just as interested in local folk bands such as Lumps of Plum Pudding from Chelmsford, named after a dance. His favourite venue was the Blue Boar at Prittlewell on Tuesdays, the Folk Song Club night. The family who ran this were involved in the English folk revival and also took over a club at Benfleet, the Hoy and Helmet, which moved again after 1970.

Twice a year there would be a ceilidh at the Oakwood in Rayleigh Road, a special event in the folk calendar. There was always an energetic caller accompanying the featured band, which would normally comprise fiddle, guitar, melodion (like the accordion), concertina, and possibly a trombone or a banjo. John eventually found his singing voice with the local folk club, but this was not until the 1970s.

In the meantime, it was from the Far East that the competition eventually came that forced EKCO to join up with Pye, and the group was eventually taken over by Philips Electrical. Exports were hived off, some of the staff were moved to Rochford, and severance arrived for John in 1968 because he did not want to move to Croydon and leave his mother, who had been widowed in 1966.

JUNE WINKWORTH

Keeping Fit

June started the 1950s and secondary school at about the same time. Up to 1951 she was at West Leigh Juniors, and living in a rented bungalow by Belfairs Woods in Leigh-on-Sea. The bungalow's garden backed on to the Army training area and their drill hall, and June recalls the bonfire parties they had. She and her three siblings (two brothers and a sister) shared a bedroom at that stage, but had more space when they moved to a council house in Juniper Road, Leigh. Now she had only to share with her sister, Jean.

Unfortunately for the whole family, June's mum suffered for years with tuberculosis, which involved long spells in hospital, although she did recover. In

the early 1950s, she and Jean were both hospitalised in the same ward at Rochford Hospital. At this point, it was not clear if Jean had pleurisy or tuberculosis like her mother, and June helped her dad with the boys as well as cycling with him to visit her mum and sister in the hospital. June herself only recalls one stay in hospital – with scarlet fever – and that was at the Balmoral Hospital for infectious diseases, then in Balmoral Road, Westcliff. This was regarded as an essential precaution for children who had brothers or sisters.

Although June was offered a place at Westcliff High, she liked the new gym at Eastwood School and chose that in preference. This rather indicated the way her interests lay, something she shared with her grandfather, who hurdled for

Jean (left) and June Winkworth on Southend beach, 1952. (Winkworth collection)

England, and her interest in sport made a real impact on her later life. At Eastwood School, she enjoyed gymnastics and hockey, she was in the school netball team, which meant playing on Saturdays, and she also ran competitively for the school.

Of more interest than her schooldays, perhaps, are June's range of jobs. She started at the Co-op by the Woodcutters pub in Belfairs, Leigh, for £3 per week. This involved weighing sugar, cutting cheeses, cutting and shaping lard, and scrubbing all the shelves every Saturday. There were no adding machines, so she had to be adept at maths, and she had to know all the prices off by heart.

For a while, she had a job at EKCO near Priory Park, where she worked with her sister on the production line wire-dressing (ensuring television sets did not shorten), and she took part in a sports rally with them as part of their sports club activities.

She then went to Aubrey Young's, a top-class ladieswear shop in Hamlet Court Road, Westcliff, specialising in designer labels such as Jaeger and Pringle. She particularly remembers dingo-skin gloves, and sending silk stockings to be mended because it was too expensive to replace them. This area was then quite an upmarket shopping area, and the window displays were especially important – it was considered a little vulgar to display more than one or two items in the window at one time.

Next came Keddies department store in Southend High Street, where June worked in the bedding department on commission. Sales assistants had a hierarchy, which meant that the most senior (First Hand) got priority, followed by Second Hand if First Hand was busy, and Third Hand next in line, with anything left over for the juniors. A lot of June's time was spent in the stockroom and packing, so she felt it was time for another move.

Attracted by the idea of not working on Saturdays, June then took a job as a junior office girl at Bates, Son and Braby, a solicitor's in Victoria Avenue, Southend. She learned how to use the early doll's eye switchboard here, but it wasn't her forte because she kept cutting people off. The offices overlooked the bowling green, but at this stage June had no idea that she too would be playing one day, and for Essex. This green was actually taken up and moved to Eastwood Park Bowls Club in 1969 following the redevelopment of the Victoria Avenue area, the original site now an office block. The actual club was re-sited nearby at the corner of Tickfield Avenue and Tunbridge Road in the same year.

Round about this time she went to evening classes in Southend, studying book-keeping to RSA level, enabling her to extend the choice of jobs open to her. She worked for Kenning's GK Electric by Chalkwell Park for a while in stock records but found that monotonous, and then moved to John Blundell's, a credit firm, as an assistant clerk.

Sport, however, had certainly not taken a back seat. While at her first job (the Co-op) June met the man who organised the Hadleigh Olympiads, and she joined the club as a youngster, competing against such clubs as Southchurch Park Running Club and doing well with her running, and in the high jump and long jump. She went on her pushbike to the cinder track in John Burrows Park, Hadleigh, on which she sported spiky running shoes. Solby's House, in the park's grounds, was then used as a changing room, and is now a privately owned dwelling. In 1956, June went up to Pleshey, near Chelmsford, with the Olympiads, and beat the legendary Mary Rand in the 100yd dash. (Mary was of course the first British woman athlete to win gold in the long jump at the 1964 Tokyo Olympics.)

When not competing, June had another physical interest – jiving. The Kursaal, when it featured Kenny Ball, Kenny Baker or Jack Parnell particularly, was a favourite place for this, as well as Mimi Green's in London Road. The Queen's Hotel in Hamlet Court Road was more classy, with its luxurious decor including some spectacular velvet curtains, and its dress code. She and her husband-to-be, Ted, won jiving heats locally, progressing to winning a number of cups in London finals.

Thomas Brothers store, Southchurch Road, c. 1960. (Nicholls collection)

June (with the mop of blonde hair, right) and the Keep Fit Association doing their thing at Cecil Jones School, c. 1969. (Winkworth collection)

Marriage at the early age of 18 curtailed June's activities only marginally. The marriage was at St Cedd's Church in Bridgwater Drive, and the young couple rented a flat in Northview Drive for a while before progressing to a council flat in Southend. He was an ex-merchant seaman, working as a market trader, and he became a 'Toby Man', allocating stalls in markets all over the south-east. Away from work, Ted also enjoyed bowls and snooker, so much so that June always knew where to find him when he went missing.

In 1959 their son Robert was born, but thanks to the services of local child-minders June mainly managed to continue working. One Italian lady in Meteor Road, Westcliff, had a pink room for the baby girls to sleep in, and a blue one for the boys. June claims it was her influence that hooked Robert on spaghetti for life.

She got a new job at Hugh Wyllie in London Road, Westcliff (another buy-on-credit company), as managing clerk, and had to be careful when checking the money that the tallymen, or canvassers (who sold goods door to door), collected, because any shortfall came out of her wages. Her record-keeping included a code for customers that they wanted to avoid – DS which meant 'don't serve'. Perhaps inevitably she also left Wyllie's after an argument with the manager when she had been trying to do her own and someone else's work for a week with no recompense. This resulted in her throwing the accounting books at him, although he did try and win her round later, to no avail.

Next came Snuggie Shoes on the Grainger Road Industrial Estate at Shoeburyness – another short-lived spell as their book-keeper dealing with export orders – but by 1960, she had finally found herself a long-term position, with Thomas Brothers department store in Southchurch Road (opposite where Frankie and Benny's restaurant is now). This job lasted an impressive twenty-five years.

Thomas Brothers was in competition with Keddies in the High Street, and was still utilising the overhead cash containers on pulleys, which were used to send June the payment for goods, upon receipt of which she could send back the change. She dealt with all the book-keeping, the clothes clubs and some secretarial duties, and ended up running the financial side. The discount they offered for clothes for Robert came in very handy. In 1964, around the time that Keddies stepped up their foothold in the town by opening Supa-Save, Thomas Brothers moved to Hadleigh, and June went with them.

June also found the time to teach trampoline at evening classes at Cecil Jones High School for a while, and then she joined the Keep Fit Association, where she received her formal training to teach keep-fit. Demonstrations of keep-fit by the Southend District Association were staged at the Cliffs Pavilion, Westcliff, and at one time the SDA had fifty teachers in the area. These teachers taught mainly evening classes at the schools in and around Southend, and some also managed some private tuition. The KFA organised large-scale annual rallies at the Cliffs Pavilion, booking the venue a year in advance. Her involvement also meant the occasional weekend away, especially as she progressed to training teachers herself. Mum or Ted was willing to babysit Robert on these occasions.

It was during the 1960s that Robert was growing up, of course. He went to Temple Sutton as a junior, and June became an active member of the PTA. It was the PTA who raised enough money (through fêtes and such) to have a swimming pool built there, which is still in use. Robert also began to develop an interest in sport, especially football, and later cross-country. As they had no garden, the two of them favoured spending time in Priory Park when he was a toddler, with an occasional visit to the Pier, or the market in Southend.

Sport has continued to play an important part in June's busy life. In fact, the whole family joined the Southend Bowls Club at the start of the 1970s (mainly, it has to be said, for the social life it promised), and her husband and brother went on to represent Essex, emulating her example.

KEN BROWN

Schooling, Selling and Spectator Sports

Ken was just 7 years old at the start of the 1950s, living with his mum and dad (Marjorie and Arthur) at 21 Crowstone Road, Westcliff, which was then a five-bed guest house. His parents had always been attracted to the idea of a bed and breakfast place, with Mum doing the cooking and Dad just about everything else. But after a few years, things did not really seem to be going that well, as the hotel register (which Ken still retains) evidences. Most of the guests seem to have been relatives, all of whom were given a discount.

Before 1951, when they put this experience behind them, Ken recalls that neither his mother nor his father could bring themselves to kill the chickens that they reared, and they had to pay the butcher to kill and pluck them. Another memory is of the displays of coloured minerals that were sold to guests at 6*d* a bottle. He always wanted to try one of these bottles but was never given the opportunity. One other thing, or rather person, he remembers was the cleaner, an Irish lady by the name of Pat, who was not the most efficient of employees. On one particular occasion she oiled the hall carpet with O'Cedar oil, instead of the wood flooring, misunderstanding Marjorie Brown's instructions.

From Crowstone Road, the family downsized to a smaller house in Shakespeare Drive, Southend, backing on to what is now Roots Hall football ground. Ken went to Westborough Junior School for a couple of years, walking to school past Wilkins the dairy near the junction of West Street. Wilkins made their own ice-cream, and a treat was a coconut milk ice lolly on a stick, which cost a penny or two. Nearby, a sweet shop sold penny drinks

Ken Brown's guest-house home in Crowstone Road, c. 1950. (Brown collection)

The kitchen of the guest house, c. 1950. (Brown collection)

from cooling plastic containers, one a gaudy red and one a bright green, the colours holding a strong appeal for the local children.

At Westborough, short trousers were uniform winter and summer alike. These featured in one anecdote of Ken's on the subject of an examination that was taking place, which had to be undertaken in complete silence. The only problem was that Ken felt sure the boy in the next seat had taken his pencil. Upon asking him to return it, although in a whisper, he was told to stop talking and get on with his work – an impossible task without the pencil. More whispering, which included a flat refusal from the accused boy, resulted in Ken being called out to the front of the class to receive two slaps on his bare thigh with a ruler. His pleas were ignored, so the whispering continued apace, and he was called out again for a further four whacks, reducing him to tears. This time he had to rub the injured leg which was smarting seriously, and this action revealed the pencil sticking out of his long grey sock! He had forgotten he had put it there. But why did the teacher not point it out? It still rankles.

Ken in Old Leigh, c. 1951. (Brown collection)

The hall of the guest house, c. 1950. (Brown collection)

The deserted natural amphitheatre that would become Roots Hall was known locally as the Pit. It was used to park the overflow of coaches carrying day trippers to Southend seafront, and was sometimes busy into the evening, especially during the illuminations. This was a good place for local boys to place hide-and-seek. However, it did have one downside: The Pit Gang. These were a gang of local lads, who were more reputation than action by all accounts, but whom it was best to avoid just in case. Ken remembers some of their 'names' – Squeaker, Squawker and Kipper.

Arthur Brown secured a job as a progress chaser with E.K. Cole locally after the family moved house. Soon after, in 1952, Ken's brother Alan was born at Rochford Hospital. Ken was dispatched to relatives in Watford in thick snow (this was at the end of March) for the duration, confinements being rather lengthier then than now. He still has a letter written home during this period (using his Shakespeare Drive address because he couldn't remember the Watford one), when it seems that he was looking forward to seeing his dog Gypsy, or Gyp, as much as his new brother. He found this letter after his mother had died, and it is now one of John's precious possessions.

A year later, Dad got a good deal on a television (from EKCO) in time for the coronation. It had a large magnifying glass fitted in front of a small screen, and was set in a crate-sized wooden cabinet. All the neighbours crowded in to see the special event.

It was also round about this time that Ken remembers a couple of older, neighbouring lads (one curiously called Busty) knocking on his door after he had gone to bed to ask his mum if he wanted to accompany them to see *The Belles of St Trinian's* being premiered at the Gaumont in Southchurch Road. With his parents' blessing, he got out of bed again and joined them on the bus.

Ken (right) with mother Marjorie and young brother Alan on Chalkwell seafront, 1953.
(Brown collection)

One of the reasons he liked to go to bed early was so that he could get up early in the morning to take Gyp for a walk in Priory Park. This was particularly important around October time, especially if it was windy, because he could secure the best conkers before any of the other boys got there. The dog, a mongrel, sported a harness rather than a lead, not uncommon then.

Ken's secondary education was at Fairfax School from 1954. He could see the trolley buses from his bedroom on the other side of the Pit, passing St Mary's Church in Victoria Avenue. When he saw the one he needed to catch to school, that was the signal for him to grab his satchel and fly out of the door.

It seems that the family got wind of the fact that the Pit would soon be a football ground again, so they moved to a two-bedroom bungalow in Hawkwell Road, a quiet area backing onto the railway with its steam trains. As a result of this move, Ken changed schools and went to Rochford Secondary Modern in Rocheway, now a community centre. Incidentally, he was one of only two boys to wear short trousers winter and summer at this school, and when the other boy succumbed, like the others, to long trousers, he was left to carry the flag for shorts on his own. Not that he did this willingly, because he was teased something rotten as a result, and the battle to get his parents to buy him long trousers will always be with him.

Schooldays here were particularly memorable for what seemed to be an emphasis on gardening. Each boy had an individual allotment to look after, and in the school holidays they could go in to reap the benefit of their personal harvest. Ken's Web Wonder lettuces turned out especially well. The school also had an area for soft fruit, which would be ripening as the summer holidays started. Volunteers were plucked out of the science class by the gardener to pick the blackcurrants and other fruit, with no objections from the science teacher. This environment initiated Ken's continuing interest in gardens.

Equally memorable was his first-form teacher, a vintage spinster with an obvious wig, which no one was brave enough to comment on, and who shall remain anonymous to spare her blushes, albeit from beyond the grave. Ken was a milk monitor at this time, and the crated milk had to be collected by individuals in a strict rota. This same teacher would call out a sequence of instructions, such as 'Row two, home on four' which meant that all the children in the second row of desks (the desks being in four rows with gangways between each row) should pick up a bottle of milk and a straw and return to their desks via gangway four. This was repeated every morning without variation, and very successfully it seems, the end result being that everyone was sitting down with their milk without any pushing, breakages or confusion.

In the summer, Ken cycled home to lunch, but stayed for school dinners on cold winter days, dinners that he feels did not merit the bad press associated with them. The ice-cream van, Valente, would park outside the school grounds at lunchtime, and Milo, the operator, also tried to tempt the boys with toffee apples.

While still at school, Ken developed an interest in three other directions – Elvis, football and speedway. Elvis records were played on a bulky radiogram at home – an EKCO product, of course – in spite of Dad's protestations. The purchase of 78s was financed in part by an early morning paper round, which paid about 15s per week. The bike Ken used for this task cost approximately 16 guineas, and was a handmade McLean.

Westborough School photograph, 1954, Ken in front, far right. (Brown collection)

He saw his first floodlit football game at the new Roots Hall stadium in 1956 and was hooked; he has supported Southend United ever since. In the late 1950s, the stadium was all-standing, and the supporters (many of them family groups) stood, naturally, behind their team's goal. However, they were not kept separate from the competition's supporters, and at half-time the supporters at each end changed places, with no more than a little joshing as they passed each other.

The team Ken supported at the Rayleigh speedway (where Sainsbury's is now) was the local team, the Rayleigh Rockets. The key place for fans was on the first all-action bend, and regulars had clipboards to keep a record of the scores on the programmes. Some of these clipboards were painted with the Rockets' colours: purple, if his memory serves him right. They used to chant:

> ONE, TWO, THREE, FOUR
> LET US SEE THE ROCKETS SCORE
> R–O–C–K–E–T–S
> ROCKETS!

A favourite rider was Reg Reeves, who was known as the Gay Cavalier of Rayleigh Weir as a result of his beard and moustache (and not for any other reason). The entrance fee was a couple of shillings, perhaps half a crown, and it seems to have been even more family oriented than the football. Ken did have quite a nasty accident one evening on the way back from speedway, when his bike was caught in a car bumper and dragged along the road, but fortunately it was only the bike that was a write-off.

When Ken left school in 1958, he had rather assumed that his dad would be able to get him a job at EKCO, but it did not happen. So he applied to a few shops and was taken on by Keddies department store in Southend High Street as a junior sales assistant in the hardware department. His starting wage was £3 5s per week, rising to £3 10s after three months. His three years here seem to have been exactly like the portrayal in *Are You Being Served?* (the 1970s sit-com). There was certainly a dandified floorwalker with a red carnation, and his hands behind his back, who was lord and master of all he surveyed. A strict hierarchy was observed, no doubt because of the amount of commission that could be earned. Juniors were not allowed to serve unless their seniors were busy. Even then, if a junior looked like securing a sale of a bulkier item such as a refrigerator, a senior would intervene and take the sale over. The manager, who had a key to the till, would open it up several times a day to see whose code numbers had been entered alongside the various sales, and if your number was there a little too often you were known as an Old Grabber. So poor old Ken spent much of his day doing a prodigious amount of dusting.

It was a bit of a standing joke within the department that if a customer wanted something delivered, especially if it was something they could easily carry themselves, then they must be from Thorpe Bay, which had a reputation for well-heeled residents at the time. Keddies' delivery van was a distinctive green, on a par perhaps with Harrods.

While at Keddies, Ken learned a lot about the retail business, about sales, and about china, especially Royal Doulton. Mrs MacGregor, known as Mac, was a bit

Ken at Keddies' Christmas grotto, 1951. (Brown collection)

of an expert when it came to china, and happy to pass on all she knew. The store also had its own social club, and day trips for the staff were organised on an occasional Sunday. The most memorable was a trip to Stratford-upon-Avon, but the driver got lost and they ended up spending most of the day on the coach, with a brief stop in Bath. They never got to Stratford.

The highlight of the Keddies year was the Christmas grotto. Everyone, including the juniors, would be involved in getting it set up. It took up half the basement area, with an electric train of about five carriages that took the paying customers on a well-planned tour. In return for what could have been a long wait in the queue, they were treated to a vista of snowmen, decorations, winter scenery, with the bells ringing out, culminating in a visit to Father Christmas who presented all the children with a gift.

The longest queue, however, was probably when Keddies opened Supa-Save at the back of the store in 1964, replacing the Strand cinema. Ken has the brass knocker from the door of the Strand's manager's office as a souvenir! He was on duty on opening day, allowing the crowds in a few at a time to avoid a stampede. No one in the UK had had the American experience of walking round and helping themselves to what was on display, paying only when they were finished shopping. Add to that the discounted prices and they were on to a winner.

Socially, in the late 1950s Ken had learned to jive, although he thought the Long Bar, the rock 'n' roll venue in the Palace Hotel at the top of Pier Hill, was a bit on the sleazy side. The Victor Sylvester dance studio above the Odeon in Southend High Street was more his cup of tea. One evening a week was beginners' ballroom night, and, to ensure no one was left without a partner, the idea of a 'chair dance' was initiated. The chair was at one end of the dance floor; girls lined up one side, and boys the other, and as you got to the chair, you paired off. Ken remembers that as he got near to the front of the line, he started to count, and if he did not like the look of the girl that he would end up with, he would change his place in the line-up. As no doubt he was not the only one doing this, the chair dance may not have worked quite as intended.

Victor Sylvester's closed at 10.30 p.m., and Ken and his friends would move on to the bowling alley at the entrance to the Pier, which was open all night. It was not licensed, but it did serve coffees and food. In fact, if you booked three games between 11.30 p.m. and 1.30 a.m. you got a free breakfast.

By the early 1960s, Ken's hopes of management training at Keddies did not seem to be advancing, so he went to work for Williams and Howard, the paint manufacturer next to the Cricketers in London Road, Southend. His job title was now management trainee, but again he was more of a dogsbody, although for better money. The company was a wholesale and retail supplier, and had a warehouse at the rear with huge drums of paint, which were fairly hefty for young Ken to move around. He did get a chance to work in the shop on occasion, as well as in the plant.

The year 1963 turned out to be a life-changing one. It was the year he met Marian while she was walking her dog in Hockley Woods. Marian was to become Mrs Brown, but in the meantime she persuaded Ken to try for a job in London; she was working there, in a bank. So he took a day off to visit some London agencies, and one of them arranged an interview for him at Continental Express (Transport) opposite the Old Bailey. He was taken on as a junior clerk in the shipping department at £9 per week, ending up as air freight manager after a few years. This job was particularly convenient as Marian worked nearby and they could meet up for lunch a couple of days a week. This cost around half a crown, paid for with their luncheon vouchers. His season ticket to London was around £17 for three months.

Marian is the eldest of five children, with strict parents who made sure she was in by 10.30 p.m., even when she and Ken had been dating for several years. He finally plucked up the courage to talk to her dad about marriage, having been advised that he would have formally to ask for permission. Marian's dad's main concern was apparently Ken's earning capacity, but, although on £15 per week by then, he seems to have just scraped by in the suitability stakes.

They married in 1967 at Hawkwell Church, with a reception at Hawkwell Village Hall. There was no dancing, but there was a record player for music. The food was a buffet spread to speed up the process, because the hall closed promptly at 6.30 p.m., just five hours after the time they had booked for their wedding ceremony. After a Devon honeymoon, the couple lived in a mobile home on the Hockley Mobile Home Estate while they saved up for a deposit on their own house. They splashed out occasionally, however, on frothy coffee or lemon tea at the Sorrento in Southend High Street near the junction with Pier Hill.

This venue had a jukebox with a television screen above that featured different video performances, not linked to the record that was playing. But it was not unusual if you liked to watch, for instance, the Pamplona bull run incident when the doors to the bull ring jammed and several men were crushed by the bulls, to choose the record that went with that particular video, rather than choose the record for its own sake. Apparently, all the videos were similarly gruesome. Ken, however, did not lose his taste for the more refined atmosphere of Victor Sylvester's, except that now he was accompanied by his wife.

In 1970, the couple finally made it to their own bungalow, a semi-detached in Southview Road, Hockley, with a 200ft garden: plenty of room for the essential chickens, though these were for eggs, not for killing. By now, Ken's father had progressed to making wine, and Ken still has the detailed log he kept – times certainly were a'changing for the Browns.

SUE COX

A Life Touched by Drama, Music . . . and Pets

S
ue was born in 1945 in the family home at Walsingham Road, Southend, fifteen years after her sister, Beryl. Their parents were originally from London, and Mum still, in the 1950s, sported a turban over her curlers until the afternoon. Dad drove for Red Lion Petrol, which eventually became Esso, delivering fuel to heavy users such as airfields. Although Sue does remember her first year at Bournemouth Park School in 1950 – principally because of the shed-type structure that first-year pupils mainly studied in – she does not recall being a bridesmaid at her sister's wedding in 1951.

Early memories strengthen from around 1953, a significant year for many reasons. There was the coronation – with a gift of a suitably decorated mug from school – and the funeral of a cousin who had been an Army officer and lived nearby, with its gun carriage, the plumed black horses and the Union Jack draped over the coffin. Then there were the floods, in which her brother-in-law was involved as a helper. Sue was diagnosed with double pneumonia just as the floods hit the area, and as a result of the influx of victims at local hospitals, there was no room for her as an inpatient. Her treatment was therefore at the hands of her GP and her family, though the outcome was completely successful. For her brother-in-law, life was more ephemeral. He sadly died a few months later following a tragic accident, and her sister returned to the family home.

Before her marriage, Beryl had been a window dresser at Keddies in Southend High Street. Sue remembers visiting Dixons in the High Street (a department store, where W.H. Smith is now) to ride on their rocking horse, and then visiting Beryl at Keddies and admiring the displays. Beryl's job meant that Sue benefited from such goodies as a brand-new doll and a blue pushchair from Keddies' toy department, when up to that point everything had been second hand.

The family home was a bungalow with a big garden, built by Sue's uncle and offered to her father for a bargain price: a £25 deposit and £500 in return for decorating the place. The road was not made up at the time, but there was the luxury of an inside toilet and a tin bath. On the end of the tin bath, to heat up the room, a Tilley lamp was perched precariously. The floors were covered with lino with a few carpet strips called runners, but there were some primitive electric pipes rigged up behind Sue's bed to provide a modicum of heating. In the garden, Sue's dad took responsibility for the chickens and for growing

Bournemouth Park School photograph, 1953. Sue Cox is in the back row, second from right, and Mrs Ross is the class teacher. Note the coronation hats. (Cox collection)

vegetables, and Mum was warned off if she interfered: her role was very much indoors.

The family were Salvationists, and the citadel they attended is still in Clarence Road, Southend, although there was also one in Southchurch. Dad played the cornet, and Beryl was also musical. They had a piano at home, and this was Beryl's speciality. Sue herself attended the open-air concerts given by the band, and joined in on the tambourine on occasion. She went to meetings on Sunday with many other members of their extended family, and there were several uncles and cousins who were part of the uniformed band. Sue herself, however, admits to a slight preference for the music of the Everly Brothers and (later) Paul Anka. Sundays were also memorable for *Meet the Huggetts* and *Life with the Lyons*, popular 1950s radio comedy 'soaps'.

As the 1950s progressed, Dad may have had trouble finding the money for the uniform that was required, because he seems to have stopped being so involved with the Salvation Army and at around the same time he had to get a different job when Esso came into being. He became an insurance agent, and Sue used to help him by delivering leaflets through doors. By now, the family had managed to buy a Ford Popular, and they were fast acquiring pets – rabbits and a dog. Sue's uncle in Ferndale Road, Southend, promoted her lifelong interest in animals because Sue often visited him and his parrot, his rabbits and his Pomeranians, among others. Sue also visited her grandma in Guildford Road, and liked outings to Southchurch Park to feed the ducks.

Sue's senior school was Wentworth, now Cecil Jones. She liked art and was often top of the class in this subject, but she was also interested in netball, literature, history and needlework. This latter interest she could develop at home because the family had a manually operated Singer sewing machine.

The first memorable job Sue had after leaving school was with the new Supa-Save in Warrior Square, part of the Keddies complex. This was Britain's first retail discount store, and Sue worked there briefly, packing eggs, something she did not enjoy or feel to be of great merit. Soon after, she found her feet at the town's biggest employer, EKCO in Eastern Avenue, Southend, where she started off doing filing, and then typing. There were as many as forty-six typists in the pool, and although everyone smoked this was not an issue and the atmosphere was cheerful and usually busy (though Sue admits that for less taxing moments she had her knitting in the drawer). A lot of time was spent on the messy and inky Gestetner machine, an early method of producing numerous copies for distribution to the many departments and factories – the latter in Prittlewell, Charfleets, and as far as Malmesbury. By 1969, however, the typing pool had been cut by more than half, and EKCO gradually downsized.

Sue became quite versatile at work. She was called upon to walk along the railway track on occasion to collect reams of paper from the stationery department; she was asked to help out in the wages department; and she was

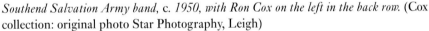

Southend Salvation Army band, c. 1950, with Ron Cox on the left in the back row. (Cox collection: original photo Star Photography, Leigh)

The EKCO typing pool, c. 1962, with Sue (wearing glasses) hidden in the centre. (Cox collection)

involved in producing some of the private documents that made sensitive references to such subject matter as radar. A less happy connection with EKCO was being knocked down by a car outside the premises, which saw Sue having forty stitches in her face, lips and tongue.

It was while working at EKCO at the beginning of the 1960s that Sue met her lifelong best friend, Lesley Brown. The girls were soon planning their first week's holiday abroad together – and their first flight, from Southend airport to Jersey. But because money was tight, they planned on sleeping one night at Jersey airport – until Sue's dad found out. He then proceeded to book a farmhouse for them for one night, so their holiday could go ahead and Sue could stock up with cheap Peter Stuyvesant ciggies. She even managed to find the money for a weekly shampoo and set at Vogue's in Southend.

The two teenagers enjoyed the many coffee bars in Southend in the 1960s – the Capri, Zanzibar and the well-known (for its live bands) Shades. They also enjoyed the Goldmine, and dancing at the London Hotel and at the Victor Sylvester Studios in the High Street. Occasionally, the girls went to the EKCO Club House, although it was only the Christmas get-together that particularly appealed. Sue also went to see wrestling at the Kursaal occasionally with her sister

Sue (left) and best friend, Lesley Brown, at Southend airport, c. 1962. (Cox collection)

The EKCO staff dance at the Kursaal, 1963. Left to right: Ros Powell, Helen Dunn, Susan ?, Kath Powell, Sue and Lesley Brown. (Cox collection: original photo Hamlet Court Studios, Westcliff)

GOMEZ MAXIMILLIANO

BOLLETT v. ZARANOFF | Howes v. Wiricogha | MURPHY v. MORICE | SZAKACS v. MIQUET | Kovacs v. Da Silva | Borienko v. Fury

Wrestling programme from the Kursaal, 1964. (Smeeton collection)

and brother-in-law (Beryl remarried in the 1960s). One of the regulars was an Australian, Bill Verna, who was a family friend.

It was at yet another coffee bar, the Woodpecker in Clifftown Road, that Sue met Andrew, who was a year older than herself. He worked as a central-heating engineer and lived with his parents in one of the cottages in Coleman Street, Southend, now flats. Andrew was one of the many who queued all night for Beatles' tickets in 1963 at the Odeon, but the general consensus was that their concert seems to have been blotted out by the screaming of the fans.

The bill for Sue's wedding ring, July 1965.
(Cox collection)

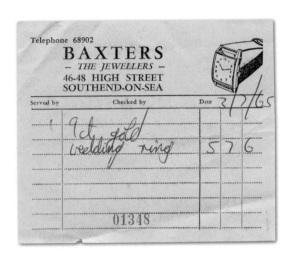

Telephone 68902
BAXTERS
— THE JEWELLERS —
46-48 HIGH STREET
SOUTHEND-ON-SEA

Served by	Checked by	Date 3/7/65
1	9ct gold wedding ring	5 7 6

01348

Two years later, in 1965, the couple were married at St Luke's Church in Bournemouth Park Road, a small wedding with the reception at Sue's home and a wedding dress made by Beryl. After a few days in Kent, they lived in a small first-floor flat in South-view Drive, Westcliff, with the landlord downstairs. One of Sue's earliest house-keeping mistakes was to polish the lino under the rugs, which sent the two of them sprawling on a few occasions.

Soon they moved to a rambling three-storey house in Stanley Road. This seemed to them quite a noisy area initially, especially in the season, with many families in the fishing industry living nearby, but they soon got used to it. It had been left empty when a friend's mother – who used to let out the rooms – died, and Sue and Andrew rented the ground floor. However, the whole place was a bit daunting for Sue – it always seemed to be damp, there was still gas lighting, and the place was creepy and dark, especially as it was empty upstairs. She used to leave a casserole in the oven with a very low light when she went out, but just the unexpected pop of the gas when she returned was enough to frighten her out again. What happened to the casseroles is long forgotten. Specific memories of that period are of using a flat iron, and of plugging in their small television into next door's electricity at a cost of just a few shillings a week!

To help them save for their own house, the couple earned money in the evenings by taking on decorating jobs at the end of their working days. Sue has always been a bit of a sucker for animals, and while in Stanley Road, they acquired a stray black cat, Binky, found outside the EKCO offices, and a grey poodle, Lulu, which Andrew's mum found. Later Sue saved another puppy, Susie, from being put to sleep by giving her a home, too.

They eventually saved enough for a deposit on a bungalow in Sherbourne Gardens near Southend airport in 1966, when the area was very rural. It cost around £3,300 but needed a lot of work. Eventually, Sue managed to get a vegetable garden going and really enjoyed making her own jam and chutneys.

Nicholas, their son, was born in 1969 at Rochford Hospital, necessitating a forceps delivery. Sue spent fourteen days recuperating back at her mum's home after the birth, not unusual in the 1960s.

As a postcript, Sue was given a Brightwell's Bakelite clock in recent years. This came from the store in the High Street that specialised in fabrics, and was – with its unusual pull-down winder – a feature of the interior. It was a present from a friend whose father worked there many years ago and is a nostalgic reminder of times past.

ROGER GLOVER

Still Rocking

Roger is a baby-boomer, born in North Avenue, Southend-on-Sea. His nan was a local midwife, Dad worked at the brick fields in Wakering, and his mum worked part-time for a while on the production line at EKCO. He and his three sisters were all born in the same room, and even his mother was born in the same house.

His education started at Bournemouth Park Infants and Juniors, then Southchurch Hall High School, now Ambleside College for Further Education. He remembers getting away with not always wearing school uniform; nor was he a fan of sporting activities,which he always tried to avoid.

School lunches were at home, and his playground was the alleys at the back of the terraces. There was the ubiquitous outside loo, no electricity until 1951, a tin bath (up to the 1960s), a pushbike for transport for Dad, and Saturday nights spent at the local pub. When on a visit to Southend High Street, Roger remembers Bobin's bookshop in the Talza Arcade, or more specifically three shrunken heads in their window for some reason. He also recalls the pet shop, which sold live chicks at Easter and chickens all year round.

In the early 1950s, Roger's dad took him over the brick fields, which featured massive sand dunes, a paradise for a young boy. He 'helped' push the trolleyloads of bricks. Dad often worked on Sundays, keeping an eye on the kilns, but when they had the opportunity as a family, a favourite outing was to one of the several pubs along the seafront that sported a beer garden.

Around 1953, Dad bought the first family car, a 1937 MG saloon, and then the family's 'free' Sundays were often spent on Canvey Island, which was a quieter area then and a bit of an adventure. A couple of times a year the family also visited the Pier, and Roger can recall the sound of the Pier trains rumbling along, audible from up to 2 miles away.

As a young boy, Roger was fascinated by Tornado Smith's skill on the Kursaal's Wall of Death (a seemingly flimsy wooden upside-down cone!). Smith did warm-up demos outside the Wall as a taster, to attract people in to the full show, and performed with a couple of other riders, including a well-known female one, Yvonne Stagg. He wore plus fours and the sort of boots that people usually reserve for horseback, rather than predictable biker leathers.

In 1953, the family acquired a television from Summers in Southend to watch the coronation. Roger's uncle lived nearby in Archer Avenue, where they had a street party in the rain to celebrate the event. Soon after, Roger and his sister managed to break their precious television as a result of some rough-and-tumble, and Dad became one of the first customers at Radio Rentals in Southchurch, renting a television.

When Roger was 9, his cousin bought a motorbike, and that was it – Roger was hooked. He has been a biker ever since, a later influence being the American Vince Taylor, who apparently appeared with his band, the Playboys, at the old Odeon in Southend High Street when they used to have teenage shows, which replaced Saturday morning pictures. Acquisition of a motorbike had to wait, of course. Before that event, Roger was out and about with his school friends on pushbikes.

When he was 13, he read in the *Southend Standard* that a coffee bar, the Zanzibar, was opening off Southchurch Road, and he could not wait to visit. It had stairs disappearing down into darkness, with red Rexine seats with white piping, a Gaggia coffee machine, ten-pin bowling at the back, and an orange-squash machine with seemingly plastic oranges floating on the top of the moving liquid. This club was for teenagers only, although there were a few youth clubs in the area in the 1950s, mainly associated with churches – for example, the Bellevue Youth Club in Bellevue Road.

Two years later, Roger left school and found himself a job in the local paper as a furrier's apprentice with Jules Gee opposite St Mary's Church (where Churchill Gardens is now), earning £3 10s per week. During this period, Roger learned to prepare skins – mainly musquash – by cutting out defects and holes, and stretching them, mostly for London customers. He found the overtime payable for evenings and Saturday mornings very useful. When this extra money was eventually stopped about 1965 as the trade declined, he left and took a job in the building trade, starting as a labourer. He found he preferred outdoor employment and also worked back in the brick fields for a while. One older sister found work in a local printer's, and another worked out the dividend at the Co-op in Sutton Road.

A sum of £50 borrowed from his dad secured him his first motorbike, an Aerial Leader, at the age of 16. Roger claims that the Southend driving test centre was notorious as the most difficult area to gain a pass, and this is why he failed his test three times. The examiners gave out instructions at the beginning of the test, and *walked* round, observing the biker's skills for half an hour. But at 17, he finally had his licence, and was able to repay his dad's loan within six months.

His leathers were ordered by post from Pride and Clark in London, and paid for in instalments, but the Army and Navy stores in London Road, Westcliff, could supply gloves and accessories. Later, he discovered a handbag shop in York Road, Southend, which provided leather trims, then studs, so enabling black leather jackets to be individualised with a bit of stitching at home – his first personalisation was a horse's head, then he added sleeve 'frills' and later his name.

A lot of Roger's friends in the area shared his interest and his propensity for black leather, but they would not be served if they went into any of the mod clubs (for example, the Jacobean in Southchurch), although they had the same taste in

music at the time, such as ska, blue-beat, and rhythm and blues. Some places would not even let Roger and his friends through the door, especially if they sported the full kit: crêpe-soled chukka boots and ice-blue jeans in the 1950s, moving on to white tie, white scarf and white boots in the early 1960s. They were seriously outnumbered by mods in the area. During Whitsun 1964 mods were prevented from descending on the town by the local police force, who shut the A13 and A127 and did not allow anyone in on a scooter unless they could prove their residence. As a result there did not seem to be any serious confrontations.

A favourite haunt until around 9.30 p.m. was the Southend Youth Centre in Alexandra Street; after that they moved on to one of the numerous coffee bars with their jukeboxes. There are, however, a couple of live acts Roger remembers seeing at the time – Screaming Lord Sutch at the Pop Inn in Station Road, Westcliff-on-Sea, and Chuck Berry at the Odeon in the High Street. At home he had a Dansett record player, and bought his records (mainly old jukebox discs) from a spiv-type man who had a table at the Talza Arcade on Saturdays. These cost around 6*d* each or three for 1*s*.

The 77 Coffee Bar, near to the mod haunt of Shades in Eastern Esplanade, opened in 1962. The police often booked those who drove on or off the forecourt here, so if they arrived after Roger or his friends, the lads had to carry their bikes back into the road. One of them was able to carry it at shoulder height. The police soon became tired of their waiting game.

Zanzibar also became a biker café, and there were bikers called café racers who literally raced from one café to another, sporting their low handlebars and their set-back foot rests. One of the café areas where leather jackets were banned was the one attached to the bowling alley at the entrance to the Pier. In the 1960s, this venue was very busy twenty-four hours a day, and you had to book in advance to get a game.

For Roger, the 1950s and 1960s have never really disappeared. He is the founder of Southend Shakedown, which organises a reunion, now an international rally, every Easter bank holiday Monday along Southend seafront to bring back the heyday of the bikers. By 2005, the event had grown to sufficient prominence to be extensively featured on BBC Essex.

Roger in recent years. (Glover collection)

BRIAN AND SUE CRONK

The Mod Scene

Brian and Sue are both Southend born and bred, Brian originally from the Southchurch area and Sue from Shoeburyness. They have similar memories of home life in the 1950s. Brian's family used the public baths on the corner of Lifstan Way until they had a bathroom about 1961, and Sue remembers removing the kitchen tabletop to reveal their metal bath underneath.

Sue's nan and granddad shared the family house, including the kitchen and the outside loo, and Brian had a granddad who worked at Howard's Dairies as a milkman when they used horse-drawn vehicles. His other granddad, a miner, lived much farther afield in Wales, although he came to Southend for an occasional holiday. On one occasion, Granddad was helping in the family's nearby allotment when he inadvertently dug up a bees' nest and came running into the house with scores of stings on his bald head. These allotments are now a playing field for cricket and games.

One luxury Brian did have was a gas fridge, probably as a result of having a father who worked at the gasworks on the seafront. Gas central heating did not arrive until 1965, however.

As children in the 1950s, they attended different schools. Brian went to Hamstel Primary in Hamstel Road, while Sue went to Richmond Avenue Primary. Sue has particularly vivid recollections of childhood escapades – from throwing a tin mug across the classroom in temper, partly because she just did not like being there, to 'encouraging' a young redhead, Eileen, to have a nose bleed by bonking her on the nose so that she could get out of lessons. Not surprisingly, standing in corners featured in Sue's early school days.

When not at school, Brian and his friends enjoyed playing – somewhat riskily – on the nearby railway line. The fogs were so much thicker in the 1950s that detonators were laid on the lines to warn workmen, or whoever, that a train was approaching, something the boys found fascinating. Similarly, the bomb site, where the Cliffs Pavilion now stands, was another favoured haunt. Brian's local community used to organise trips with the Nicholls Coach Co. to places such as the Norfolk Broads or the Finsbury Park Theatre. The nearest youth club seems to have been at Caulfield Youth Club, which was also Sue's nearest, although she is a couple of years younger than Brian.

Sue Cronk with her dad on his motorbike, c. 1952. (Cronk collection)

Senior school for Brian was Southchurch Hall School for Boys, now a college, while Sue's was Shoebury High. Both schools had house points systems, but recollections seem to be more about being rapped over the knuckles with a ruler (Sue) or of canings (Brian).

Home life for Sue was family oriented, with memories of toasting bread in front of an open fire and playing cards. There was a darts board that was well used by her dad, who was in a darts team that played at local pubs. He had been a mechanic in the RAF, becoming a milkman in the 1950s and 1960s, and he had a motorbike which he took Sue out on, balanced on a cushion on the petrol tank. Brian's dad bought his first car in 1956, when there were few cars and fewer traffic lights. The dense fogs meant someone had to walk in front of the car on occasion.

While still at school, both had Saturday jobs. Sue worked at Nat's in the Talza Arcade at Victoria Circus – Southend's version of a trendy clothing shop. Brian worked at the Kursaal on the bazookas for about 5s a session, where customers paid 1s or so to have their 'bazooka' loaded with ping-pong balls and could then attempt to win a prize. He liked this job particularly because of its proximity to the lady falling out of bed (as often as people were willing to pay), and seems to have had little sympathy for the lady concerned!

Gaslight Football Club, 1963, at the Lawns sports ground, Bournes Green, Southend. Back row, left to right: Charlie Bellamy, Geoff Taylor, Ginger Davis, Derek Roberts, Jim ?, Brian, Norman Cronk (Brian's dad), -?-. Front row: -?-, Vic French senior, Jim Breakspear, Dave Bellamy, Chris Culham, Vic French junior. (Cronk collection)

Saturday morning pictures at the Odeon in the High Street also featured, and he can remember starting to buy 45s in 1959. As the 1960s hit, Sue was becoming more interested in going out with the boys who worked on the milk rounds with her dad. She had her first heels and tights at age 13.

Brian left school in 1961 and secured an apprenticeship in gas fitting at Stratford, studying at college in East Ham for five years to pass his City and Guilds. Having always been interested in football (he played for his school), he subsequently joined the gasworks' football club in Southend, named the Gaslights, and played in their team for many years. In the meantime, he became a part of the mod scene, and bought his first Lambretta 150 in 1963, followed a year

A close-up of Brian's beloved Lambretta, 1964. (Cronk collection)

Brian and mod cousin Tuppy on his Lambretta, 1965. Note his badge collection. (Cronk collection)

Left to right: Brian Cronk, Dennis Chad Hudswell, -?-, Tony Hodgson, Roy Pitcher (? at back), outside the Peter Boat, Leigh, 1963. (Cronk collection)

later by the new GT200, and made sure he had all the added essentials – lights, mirrors – which unfortunately were stolen from the scooter, which he used to park outside his home. He had 'Southend' emblazoned on the back of his parka and travelled to the likes of Brighton for mod rallies.

Sue left school in 1964 after doing shorthand and typing at school. She hated the experience of travelling to London by train for an interview, and settled for a job with Howard's Dairies in Thorpe Bay behind the counter, much to her parents' disgust at the time. However, she seems to have quite enjoyed the intricacies of boning and cutting bacon, and slicing the diverse (or so it seemed at the time) range of cheeses on offer.

This was the year that the couple met up, at the Halfway House. Sue quickly switched her alliance from motorbikes (because of her dad) over to scooters. The mod scene in Southend centred around the cellar coffee bars. A favourite was Shades on Eastern Esplanade, which could offer live music over two floors including local up-and-coming groups such as the Paramounts with Gary Brooker (later of Procul Harum). But mods were spoilt for choice. There was also the Jacobean in Southchurch Road, and the Capri, where the Last Post pub is now, in Southend, although these had jukeboxes rather than live bands.

For dancing, there was also a good choice, and not just for mods, either. There was the Kursaal ballroom, the Elms and the Cricketers. It seems that the same man owned the Capri, the Cricketers pub, and the Jacobean, and was seen around the town with his white Rolls-Royce and heavyweight bodyguards.

The appearance of the Beatles at the Odeon in Southend High Street in 1963 was a draw for mods (and others) from miles around, but Brian queued for two nights to secure four tickets. His mum brought him food to keep him going, and in return she was one of the lucky four who got to see the live act, the others being cousins. But mods also travelled a bit farther afield to see the likes of the Dave Clark Five, whom Brian remembers seeing at Basildon.

For mod clothes, the girls had Nat's in Southend. The boys frequented a tailor's in the High Street for their suedes, leathers and sharp suits.

Sue and Brian were married in 1968 at St Andrew's Church in Shoeburyness. They held their reception at Lifstan Boys' Club in Lifstan Way, and managed to save enough money to put down a deposit on their first home in Dalmatia Road, near Brian's parents. It was also in 1968 that Brian worked on the first North Sea gas conversions on Canvey and until 1974 he was often employed in London, doing some high-profile work on the houses of many celebrities in the Hampstead area, including the likes of Cilla Black. The couple look back on the 1950s and 1960s in Southend – and on the mod era – with affection.

ANNETTE FOX

Hard Times and Happy Times

The home in Chinchilla Road, Southchurch, where Annette and her siblings were brought up, was the same home that her mother, grandma and great-grandfather had all been brought up in. Remarkably, the house stayed in the family until the 1990s, yet was never owned by them. A three-bedroom terraced house, it was then heated by a solitary coal fire downstairs, with a tin bath in the scullery and lino on the floors. A few chickens in the small backyard provided eggs and the Christmas dinner during Annette's childhood.

It was Annette who was the first born, in Rochford Hospital, followed by brother Bobby in 1949. Her parents divorced soon after, and her mum remarried and had two more girls in the 1950s. Annette's stepfather, like her own father, was a sailor. Although he had recurrent bouts of malaria, he retained enough strength to be a strict taskmaster in his new role of father.

The 1952 family with sailor stepdad. (Fox collection)

Bobby and Annette with new baby half-sister, in Southchurch Park, 1954. (Fox collection)

In between marriages, Mum took in lodgers, and Annette remembers one in particular called Mary whose young daughter Jackie seems to have been disabled by an early bout of polio. Annette, Bobby and Jackie all shared a bedroom during this period. Jackie did tap-dancing and ballet in an effort to strengthen a weakened leg, and Annette can still recall her singing 'Me and My Teddy Bear' on stage when they were both very young indeed.

At the back of the nearby White Horse pub was an orchard, and at a stretch the children could just reach the apples from the enclosing wall. Once a year they would all walk to a family friend's isolated cottage at Wakering, which had the fascination of a see-saw over a log and where you could spot an occasional stoat. The countryside was very open then and known as (Red) 'Indian Country'.

Although Mum stayed at home with the family, she did earn a little money annually by pea-picking in the fields near Holy Trinity Church. One year, young Bobby made himself ill by eating the raw peas. Later, the children earned pocket money by joining in the potato-picking in the summer season in Wakering. For this event, a lorry actually picked up the families to take them to and from the fields.

The local infant and junior school was Hamstel Road, with boys and girls segregated, and a headmistress rejoicing in the name of Whiskers. A favoured activity among the girls was bead swapping, on a par with the boys' marble swapping. One of the weekly tasks here was to change and fill the inkwells on Fridays. As for bad behaviour, that would have resulted in smacked legs.

Annette Fox and Bobby with their mum, near the entrance to Southend Pier, 1952. (Fox collection: original photograph Photo Service, Manchester)

There were often specially celebrated days at school during Annette's time there (*c.* 1952–63). Annually, there was the Mayday celebration with a day of country dancing, following the election of a May queen by the children. Empire Day was the day when you wore your Girls' Brigade (or other such society) uniform to school.

Memories of the coronation are a little different. Mum at this time was working on the production line at EKCO in Prittlewell, and the company gave a party for the employees' children. This party coincided with the storms that led to the Canvey floods. As Annette could not afford the full bus fare home after the EKCO party, she got off at the stop before, with her gift of a coronation cup and saucer, but the stormy weather blew it out of her hands as she walked home. Bobby managed to hang on to his.

During school holidays and after school, Mum used a childminder in Surbiton Road, who managed to get the children to sleep in the afternoon, to make her own

The Girls' Life Brigade at the People's Mission, featuring Annette one row back, third from the right, with long hair and neat knees, c. 1954. (Fox collection)

life easier perhaps. When Annette swung on the cupboard door at Surbiton Road and broke some plates, Mum had to replace them and was not very happy about doing it. More happily, she and Mary, the lodger who also worked at EKCO, would treat the children every payday to a banana (a rare treat in the early 1950s), a small wooden jigsaw puzzle and sometimes a small jar of sweets.

The swings at the bottom of Chinchilla Road proved a less expensive pursuit for Annette, as was time spent on her bicycle. It was also good – if not necessarily clean – fun to wave at the steam trains that passed close by, up until 1954.

For a while, Annette was a member of the Sunbeams (in effect, the Salvation Army juniors), which were based in Chinchilla Road. Sunbeams wore a grey uniform with a yellow tie, and attended weekly meetings, complete with hymns. She also joined the Girls' Life Brigade, but their different church leanings meant that it was not acceptable for her to be in both, so she continued with the GLB. This provided her with a social life at a young age, including Sunday-school sessions. That said, she was subject to the limitations of her strict stepfather, such as having to be home no later than ten minutes after the end of the GLB meetings.

Christmases at the GLB's Sunday school in the Dalmatia Mission were particularly memorable for their magnificent trees. These were decked out with a number of rag dolls, all different and all made locally. Annette coveted the fairy or the bride doll year after year, but she never got it. When the GLB moved to Belle Vue Road Baptist Church, she progressed to joining in the singing for shows that were put on for parents.

As the 1950s progressed, things were looking up at home. The first fitted carpet, a Cyril Lord, made its appearance, and from the age of 12, Annette was able to use the public baths on the corner of nearby Lifstan Way. This was when a woman was employed to restrict the amount of hot water you used by operating a special key. All the family used the baths once they were old enough. Nevertheless, this was still a time of buying a bag of stale cakes for 6*d* from Baldwin's the bakers, and taking the pram to the gasworks on the seafront on Saturday mornings for a couple of sacks of coke, which then had to be pushed up the hill. Mum utilised the milkman's Christmas Club and the savings stamps that she bought at the post office, and she unpicked wool garments bought at rummage sales to reknit as clothes for the children. The only new clothes were presents at Christmas time, although shoes were always bought new. Similarly, such luxuries as bicycles or roller skates were usually also second-hand.

Bobby and Annette managed to find the money for Saturday morning pictures at the Plaza in Southchurch Road, which seemed to favour Hopalong Cassidy and Superman, along with a serial of course, and all for 6*d*. They spent 1*d* beforehand on four sweets to last them the duration. If she did not go to the cinema, Annette liked visiting the library at Southchurch Hall, now a museum. She would zoom over the footbridge on her roller skates in search of Biggles' books. Less pleasant were the trips to the clinic at Warrior Square for childhood injections and for the dentist, who used a large gas mask if work needed doing.

The carnival was an annual free treat, and she remembers sitting on the kerb along Westcliff seafront to watch it. Nostalgia lingers on for the pipers, and the carnival queen escorted by sea cadets, followed in the evening by the torchlight procession with real torches. The whole family would visit the nearby Never Never Land on carnival day, and Annette's favourites were the Teddy Bear's Picnic with the nodding heads of the teddies, the train trip that changed from daytime to night-time lighting, and Andy Pandy.

The next school for Annette was Dowsett High for Girls in Boston Avenue, Southend. The headmistress, Miss FitzSimons, was the archetypal head complete with tweeds, brogues, glasses and a scraped-back bun. She was not averse to using the cane across the hands on occasion.

At this school, students could earn merit marks for proficiency or, its opposite, orderly marks. These marks were revealed in front of all the school, and students were either clapped or shamed by such announcements. Annette was in Cavell house, and can clearly recall the mauve badge and the tassel on her uniform beret. Other houses were Nightingale, Seacole, Fry, Curie and Keller. The rest of the uniform comprised grey jumper, skirt and tie, with no heels or jewellery allowed, and in the summer a yellow dress with white spots; most of this could be bought at second-hand sales held at the school. Memories remain

Annette outside her Chinchilla Road home, wearing the Dowsett High uniform, 1961. (Fox collection)

of the steel tips put on the toes of winter shoes so that they would last just that bit longer.

In 1961, Annette's family struggled to finance a school holiday to Switzerland, a journey made by train and boat. They even raised £5 spending money for the week. Another school holiday was to Scotland, but these are the only holidays Annette can remember having before leaving school.

She went straight from school to the china and tinware department of Woolworths in 1962, working in the stockroom. As her stepdad had now departed the family home, she treated herself to a pair of high heels with mink on the toes, but these proved to be too uncomfortable to wear at work. Her first wage was £4 per week, and out of this she bought her mum flowers and chocolates every Friday after being paid. While at Woolworths, Annette was lucky enough to win a raffle prize of tickets to see the Beatles at the Odeon.

The money was better at the EKCO factory in Eastern Avenue, Southend, although the hours were from 8 a.m. to 6 p.m. (5 p.m. on one day a week). But there was no excuse for being late because the EKCO hooter that went off in the early mornings could be heard all around the town. Annette enjoyed the job, soldering tuning units for television sets, because of the camaraderie of the girls whom she worked with. She also enjoyed the twice-daily visit of the tea-lady with tea and cakes. Not so pleasant was the ritual involved if you were too ill to continue working. You had to see a foreman who issued you with a ticket to leave, if convinced of the genuine nature of your illness.

Socially, life was busy in the 1960s in Southend for Annette and her friends. A favourite was dancing at the dance hall next to the Cricketers in London Road, which featured live jazz on Monday nights, and frequenting the many coffee bars such as the Jacobean or the Capri with their basement jukeboxes, their espressos, and their see-through cups and saucers. Additionally, she enjoyed the live music and dancing at the Halfway House on the seafront on Fridays and Saturdays, with the Black Cat coffee bar next door. Her favourite cinema was Garons in Southend High Street. In the summer, bottle parties were all the rage.

In the meantime, Annette's mum was working in pubs to supplement the family income. One of her favourite bargains was to visit the butcher's in the Talza Arcade at Victoria Circus and buy enough meat for the week for 10s, including a leg of lamb, ox tongue and lamb hearts.

It was in a seafront pub that Annette met her first husband in 1966. They married in 1967 at Holy Trinity Church. This was when Annette had her first bathroom, in the flat they moved into in Baxter Avenue. Her husband was a pipe fitter who worked away and came home at weekends. But it was Annette who was better able to hang on to the money that came in to pay the rent and the bills. Brother Bobby, by the way, had become an electrician.

Other jobs Annette had in the 1960s were all in factories. Machining ties came after EKCO, then machining shirt cuffs for an American company in Benfleet. Next was the Brightwell Box Company in Southend, which made the Rexine trimmings for transistor radios and record players. From here she moved, following a supervisor she admired, to another producer of Rexine, where she was on piecework, and so earning extra money, and she worked at Marshalls, the cabinetmaker's, for a while, where her mum also worked.

All this came to an end at the same time as the swinging sixties. In 1970, Annette adopted a distantly related baby, Sharon, going through a form of private adoption formalised at the Southend Court House in front of a judge. She then gave up work and became a registered childminder for a while to supplement her income, particularly important as her divorce followed not long after.

ANGELA CALLAHAN

A Rough Start

Angela, a Southender, has a very different perspective on growing up in the town from most, because of her early family difficulties. Her poverty-stricken (and occasionally violent) parents, both with health problems, had trouble coping with little Angela and her younger brother, and in 1951, at the age of just 4, Angela was removed from her home environment by Miss Ridd, the then chief social worker of Southend. Miss Ridd, regarded by Angela obviously as a bit of a saint, provided accommodation in her own home for one night before transferring Angela and her brother to Seaview Children's Home in Ulster Avenue, Shoeburyness.

Seaview was council run, and it was a great relief for Angela to be in a place of safety. She remembers the clean, shiny floors, the dormitory she slept in, and the privacy you were accorded only if you had chicken pox or the like. She also remembers getting smacked for things that she didn't realise were wrong – eating with her hands, for instance, or wetting the bed. Miss Reed ruled the roost, and the hairbrush she used on her long plaited hair was the same one she used for giving you a whack if you didn't toe the line. Regardless of this, Angela's memories are positive, rather than negative, and she has even contacted some of her friends from that period of her life, thanks to Friends Reunited.

Soon after, Angela's brother was returned to the family home, but she was fostered. Her first foster home was in Huntingdon Road with Auntie Betty, whose husband's smoking habits put Angela off smoking for life. Another boy shared the foster home for a while, but Angela admits to being rather disruptive and she went back to Seaview for a while before moving on to Mr and Mrs Blake in Burlescoombe Road, Thorpe Bay, where she stayed for thirteen settled years. Mr Blake was a lay preacher, early retired. This was when Angela learned to read, and became very bookish as a result. The household was involved in local music clubs and local musicals and although Mrs Blake was strict, this was welcomed. The family also owned a beach hut on Thorpe Bay beach, a real luxury.

At the age of 6 Angela started her education at Greenways in Thorpe Bay, which had 'excellent school dinners'. The uniform was a black skirt, black blazer and black and red tie. She just missed her eleven-plus and went into the A-plus stream at Shoebury High School in 1958.

Angela Callahan outside the family beach hut at Thorpe Bay, c. 1959. (Callahan collection)

Now settled, the young Angela had to earn her pocket money, usually by helping 'Mum' with housework on Saturday mornings in return for 2*s* 6*d* (half a crown). A favourite haunt for Angela and her friends was the old Westcliff swimming pool on the seafront, with its top deck shaped like a boat. There were regular galas on Saturdays, a public swimming pool and a sun deck. It was a good place to listen to music (on a portable radio) and meet boys from other schools.

Saturday morning pictures was a feature of Angela's childhood and she belonged to the choir of the Ritz cinema, which travelled around to different Ritz cinemas entering competitions in places as far away as Harlow. The serials were particularly memorable, as was the free ticket you received on your birthday which was announced on stage so that everyone in the audience could sing 'Happy Birthday to You'.

As a teenager, Angela was a regular at the youth club in the local Methodist Church Hall, although her favourite reading was still *Smash Hits*. She has childhood memories of the carnival processions and especially of the Pier with its illuminations, its deck games, including quoits, and the fishermen ever hopeful at the far end.

Around the same time, she changed her method of earning pocket money by securing a job sweeping floors at John Dee's, the hairdresser's in Heygate Avenue, where the Royals is now. This meant she could afford to treat herself to stockings. Better still, Woolworths sold make-up she could afford, including Perfect Peach lipstick and see-through nail polish, which she and her friends applied in their upstairs loo. Then they would hitch up their skirts (this was after all the beginning of the 1960s) before hitting the street – very decadent.

John Dee's was a four-storey building, three above ground level and one below. The exterior was a startling black and the interior an equally startling pink. It was the largest hairdresser in the Southend area, with a mirrored reception area and sculptured plaster on the walls to emulate the look of buttoned cushions. The lower-ground floor was the staff room and the towel-drying area with large dryers. This was also where tea and coffee were brewed for clients, and stylists would ring down their orders on the internal telephone. There were five private cubicles with swing doors on the split-level first floor, with wall lights featured. These were for richer clients who paid quite a few pounds (a week's wages) to have their hair styled. The second floor was more open plan with rows of mirrors and studio lighting, the walls continuing the pink theme. At the top were more cubicles, this time without the privacy of doors.

This photograph of Queen Victoria's statue, then at the top of Pier Hill, clearly shows the Ritz cinema, 1961. (Nicholls collection)

Angela outside John Dee's hairdressers, Southend, c. 1964. (Callahan collection)

One of Angela's most difficult jobs was carrying a cup of tea from the lower floor to the top floor without spilling it in the saucer, because if Mr Dee spotted a spill he would call out 'Missy, you are stupid!' If she was taking the cup up the stairs, and Mr Dee was running down them, the chances were that his momentum would send the cup crashing to the floor. When she did break one of these precious white cups with their little gold flowers, she would have to buy a replacement out of her wages in Woolworths. Missy became Mr Dee's nickname. Or Mr Teasy Weasy. He was a perfectionist and a tad flamboyant, employing as many as twenty staff at one high point in the 1960s. All the staff wore blue nylon overalls with short sleeves, and Mr Dee personally checked all their styling work.

Angela was happy to be offered a three-year apprenticeship with Mr Dee when she left school, as such training was hard to come by. Her start wage was £1 3s 6d per week, but by the end of her apprenticeship in 1965 she was earning £8 per week. Her early training involved shadowing other stylists, and she also attended evening classes at Southend College.

During this decade the staff at John Dee learned to boil up their own conditioner, called Estolan, partly for economical reasons and partly because of the lack of availability of such products at the time. The salon advertised in the local cinema, and the staff won a number of London-based competitions – for example, for geometrical cutting.

The 1960s were a lively time for Angela in and around Southend. She queued up to buy her records at just over £1 apiece at the record shop in Weston Road, danced at the Kursaal ballroom, bought her clothes at Nat's in the Talza Arcade, and tried Chinese food at the new Flying Dragon nearby. There were plenty of places to go – the Bluebird Café, Shades on the seafront, the Black Cat next to the Halfway House, where you could spend an evening lingering over a frothy coffee. There was also the Shrubbery in Royal Terrace, a dark place with a basement, which seemed to attract hippies and dope smokers, and was rather more forbidding than the others.

She had a large group of friends, many from John Dee's, who spent time en masse at a holiday bungalow at St Lawrence Bay (a few miles north of Southend), where they took their music speakers onto the local beach. The bungalow had no toilet, so a bucket had to do for however many were there at the time.

Advert for John Dee's in Southend-on-Sea and County Pictorial, *February 1953.* (Smeeton collection)

In 1963, Angela met her husband, David, at the Elms on one of their free-for-girls nights. She had gone along with Christine, a friend from John Dee's, who knew David's brother. A favourite group at the Elms at the time was Force Five, which played a lot of Beatles' music, so much so that the pub became something of a haunt for local mods.

David's hairstyle was apparently called the Swan and was very in vogue at the time. He was a barman at the Estuary Club in Leigh-on-Sea, but later – thanks to his woodworking skills – went to work at Ballard Brothers in Hadleigh as a carpenter and shopfitter. The couple got engaged just six weeks after they met, and married when Angela was 19 and he was 20. During their engagement, Angela was living in Hadleigh, and she walked everywhere – but she still had to be home by 10.30 p.m. Their engagement ring was a second-hand purchase from Renall's in Clifftown Road – still trading there – a whopping £30 diamond solitaire. David could afford it only by not paying his mum housekeeping for quite a few weeks.

David paid for their wedding in 1966 at Thorpe Bay Methodist Church, and his mother made Angela's A-line wedding dress. They had a reception for thirty people at Garons at the top of the High Street, but could only afford to pay for the venue until 5 p.m. Angela raised the cash for a short honeymoon at the Leopold Hotel, Ostend, which involved a bumpy ride from Southend in a small, twelve-seater aeroplane. Their first home as a married couple was a caravan at Battlesbridge and their first son was born at St Andrew's Hospital in Chelmsford while they were still living there. They were then offered a council flat in Chelmsford, but these days Angela is back in her childhood haunt, Southend-on-Sea.

JIM WILLETTS

No Nitwit

Jim is Southend born and bred. He started life in Stornaway Road, Southchurch, in 1947 but remembers moving house quite a lot when he was very young. He lived variously at Manchester Drive, Carlton Avenue and Denton Avenue, all before the age of 8. These addresses were mainly council accommodation, shared with Mum, Dad, two brothers and a sister (the eldest child). Eventually, at Denton Avenue in Westcliff, the family discovered an amenable community spirit; in and out of neighbouring houses, watching the neighbours' television sets and playing outside with neighbouring children. A favourite game was marbles, although Jim was treated to a brand-new, bright-red pushbike one birthday when at junior school. In fact, such was its pristine condition that a policeman knocked at the door because he thought it was stolen.

At this time, the 1950s, Jim's violinist dad was in a well-known comedy band, the Nitwits. This meant that he travelled all around the world, and as a consequence the family did not see that much of him. If the Nitwits appeared nearer home, say at Blackpool, then Mum and one of the children would have a holiday and see him that way. Although registered envelopes containing money would turn up at intervals, there were still times when Jim and the children hid under the kitchen table and kept very quiet when the insurance man called for his weekly premium, because Mum did not have enough money to pay him.

Jim's junior school was the Prince Avenue School near to the Bell, which then boasted large playing fields. When he was just 7 or 8 years old, he used to go with his mum to the WRVS offices above Talza Arcade (now Victoria Circus) to get clothes that were only available for the poverty-stricken. This trip was made during school hours, and his mum used to send in a note explaining that he had a 'clothes fitting'. After a few of these 'fittings', to his embarrassment his teacher asked him why he could not go after school. Eventually, out of earshot of the other children, Jim had to tell the truth. Luckily, the teacher was sympathetic and the fabrication was allowed to continue as and when it was needed. Another teacher christened a jumper of Jim's acquired in this way as his 'strawberry jam jumper' as it had grey and red stripes.

The English teacher left an impression with his imaginative and scary stories, and could keep forty children spellbound. Jim particularly liked the conclusions of these stories, such as the one that ended with a boy walking past a washing line and feeling his leg grabbed by an empty sleeve 'just like I'm pulling yours'.

Kursaal amusements, c. 1959. (Photo reproduced by kind permission of Southend Museums Service)

Moving on to Eastwood High, initially a co-ed school (boys and girls were separated in the early 1960s), Jim liked cross-country. He did try football, which was an alternative to rugby on Wednesday afternoons, and clearly recalls borrowing a pair of soccer shoes with nails poking into his feet. He managed to run from one end of the pitch to another with the ball, but when he tried scoring the shoe came off and he missed out on his magic moment.

Once a week there was the youth club at the Baptist church in Hobleythick Lane, Westcliff, which featured table tennis, and introduced the 10- to 15-year-olds to music and dancing for the last hour. There was also Sunday school on occasion, and he joined the Scouts and the Boys' Brigade for a while, but nothing held his interest at this age.

At the time of local elections the children from Denton Avenue were roped in to put pamphlets through doors for the local Labour activist, and in return he would take them on a trip to Peter Pan's and Never Never Land on the seafront, with a bag of chips to follow. He had no problem recruiting child labour when such were the rewards. Never Never Land was also memorable when Jim and his family visited the illuminations once a year, as it was particularly magical when lit up at night.

From the age of 13 Jim would be able to earn 1s 3d per hour some evenings and weekends working at a garden centre in Eastwoodbury Lane near Eastwood Church, where the runway from Southend airport now encroaches. He was also the one who took on the family garden at Denton Avenue, growing some vegetables and keeping a few chickens. This may well have stimulated some interest, because, on leaving school at 15, Jim worked for a while as an assistant gardener for the Keddie family at The Lawn in Rochford; this paid £3 per week.

He was now riding a scramble bike, sold to him cheaply by a local lad, which was particularly handy to get to The Lawn, because he could use it cross-country. In fact, it was much better over grass than on the roads, as these were decidedly dangerous in the rain, although Jim did wear a helmet.

During his spell as a gardener, he learned how to skin the rabbits that had been shot in the early morning in the grounds of The Lawn. These were presented at the kitchen door in rather Victorian fashion – Jim never saw the inside of The Lawn.

On one occasion, after just a half-hour lesson, he was left alone with the sit-on lawn mower. The large grounds took a whole morning to mow, culminating in his colliding with a a prize tree and losing control of his vehicle so that the tree and the surrounding area were churned up. When he finally stopped the mower, he plucked up courage to knock at the back door and offer to pay for the damage, but Mrs Keddie was very kind and he got away with it. She also came to his rescue and drove him to the casualty department at Southend Hospital when he cut his arm on some wire badly enough to need stitches.

This was not his only mistake during his short-lived gardening career. He was supposed to burn down the overgrown wild grass in one area of the grounds, leaving the cultivated grass intact. However, it happened to be a windy day so that he spent a lot of time running around trying to beat out the quickly spreading flames with his rake, and ended up with a rather larger burned area than originally intended.

In 1963 Jim joined the Merchant Navy at the age of 16 because it seemed to offer adventure as well as double the wages. He came home to visit every three or six months, returning to Tilbury after each leave to re-sign on. Once he asked for a short trip so that he could be back in time for Christmas with the family, but ended up with his longest trip – to South America and Europe – passing the white cliffs of Dover twice, but each time being disappointed when the boat kept on going, as the recruits were never told where they were heading.

When he came home after two years, he got a taxi from the station to Denton Avenue, and was amazed to see all the new construction that was taking place around the Victoria Circus area. He brought something special back from New York: white Levi jeans and a white jean-jacket. To finish off this state-of-the-art outfit, he visited Dunn's, the gents' outfitter's and hat shop then in Southend High Street, and bought himself a white corduroy cap (*à la* Donovan). Once at home, Jim preferred the pubs to the coffee bars that had sprung up locally; the Cricketers was a favourite, with live rock music.

As to the rest of his family, older brother Fred left home at 15 and ended up working on a farm in Devon, emulating their granddad, who was a Sussex farmer.

His sister worked for a while in SMAC's when it was in Southend town centre. And his younger brother Pete, who enjoyed sailing, went to work for a sail maker's locally.

After Jim's deliberate decision to join the Merchant Navy, his next job was a more haphazard choice. He was watching some men on scaffolding putting up neon signs over some of the shops in Southend High Street. This intrigued him and he made a note of the company's phone number printed on their van, and got an interview that resulted in a job for the next five years. Although not an electrician, he worked as their mate, and was proud enough of what he was doing to visit the signs at night when they were lit, and admire 'his' handiwork. A lot of this work was along Southend seafront, with the Olympia Ballroom (then at the bottom of Pier Hill) one of the highest structures he had to work on. He also had to climb inside the 8ft metal bowling ball at the entrance to the bowling alley on Southend Pier to fix it when it stopped revolving.

The nastiest moment during this employment was when he was working at Southend airport at the top of the hangars, fitting 4ft-high letters spelling out an airline name. He was at the top of their biggest ladder (60ft tall) when the hangar doors started opening, pushed by a tractor that was supposed to sound a warning horn on approaching but that Jim was too high up to hear. He set a record sliding down the ladder before it was pushed to the ground by the hangar doors.

In 1967 Jim paid for driving lessons locally, and his first car was a bargain, even for the time – a light-blue Morris Minor for £30, sold to him by an old school friend who was emigrating. Around the same time, Jim had met and married his first wife, at St Andrews, Shoebury. Although they started married life in a caravan on a site at Rochford (where Renouf's restaurant is now), they progressed to a flat above a shop in East Street, Prittlewell, and produced two sons. He therefore had a growing family to support, and moved on for financial reasons to a firm involved in industrial and commercial cleaning and security. He became a supervisor, in charge of ten people. In a bid to keep the costs of hire staff down, Jim took on students in the summer, but this did not always pay off as he found one asleep in a school cupboard when doing a spot check.

Jim himself was doing cleaning work during the day, and earning extra money by driving a security van at night checking commercial premises. Eventually he too was guilty of falling asleep after a long night, waking up at 7 a.m., the time he was due to start the day duties 30 miles away.

During this period, Jim's mum had also been taking on some cleaning work in addition to nursing his dad, who was ill for quite a few years before finally passing away in 1968. She even managed to squeeze in some auxiliary work at the hospital, and Jim recalls her spending hours in the kitchen with the copper, the scrubbing board and the mangle. The swinging sixties did not swing for everyone, it seems.

In the 1970s, Jim married for a second time, and Frances Willetts tells her own story separately.

LESLEY HORNER

Hoofing and Hooves

Both Lesley's parents were part of Southend's public sector while Lesley and her brother, Geoffrey, grew up in the 1950s and 1960s. Dad worked as an architect for the Ministry of Works (in London prior to Southend) and Mum in medical records at Southend Hospital. The children were born at Rochford Hospital, and spent their early years in a house in Westbourne Grove, complete with tin bath and outside loo. Part of the ground floor was rented from Granddad, and Lesley shared a bedroom with her older brother and their parents until she was 7 (Geoffrey was 10). She recalled that a drawer served her as a cot for a while, although she was too young to remember this directly. Upstairs lived two old mysterious ladies behind big black curtains, and this was regarded as a no-go area.

Lesley's own grandparents lived on the first floor of a council flat in Fairfax Drive. From here she could watch the crowds coming out of Roots Hall football stadium, and would know from their faces if Southend United had won or lost. Later, she would accompany her grandparents to the Nelson at Prittlewell, where she had to stay in the lobby with a bag of crisps and a lemonade. This was a real treat.

Early memories include walking to Chalkwell Infants' School past the baker's, often pleading with Mum for a confection that looked just like a cornet with hundreds and thousands on the 'ice-cream' marshmallow topping. The Kleeneasy man called regularly selling cleaning products, and handing out tiny sample tins of polish, which Lesley delighted in. At school, Lesley developed a dislike for milk, which made her sick in those days. In the early 1950s Fairways Infants and Juniors followed, because the family moved to a new council estate in Leigh-on-Sea, on the corner of Wood Farm Close – a brand-new house, and her own bedroom; luxury indeed. The first Christmas here was very special, with an open fire, and a lot of effort expended on paper chains, the tree and decorations, and on presents. Lesley's main present that year was a pair of slippers.

Dad now commuted by train from Leigh. In his spare time, he liked to play cricket, and Lesley kept score for him at Priory Park, developing an early propensity for mathematics. Dad and Geoffrey both put in an appearance with the local Avenue Players, and Mum too got involved backstage. The whole family looked forward to the annual carnival, when the children would always enter the fancy dress – one year Geoffrey was Neptune, and Lesley was a mermaid. To see the daytime procession meant quite a long walk along Chalkwell Avenue, and the night-time torchlight procession was a very special event.

COUNTY BOROUGH OF SOUTHEND-ON-SEA EDUCATION COMMITTEE

Fairways Junior School

REPORT dated...... July 1958

ATTENDANCE...... Satis:

NAME ...... Lesley SIMS

CLASS 4A

POSITION..in age group $\frac{9}{92}$

ENGLISH				OTHER SUBJECTS			
Written English			Good.	Geography			Good.
English Language			Good.	History			Satisfactory
Reading—Oral			Fairly Good.	Nature Study			Average.
Reading—Comprehension			Good.	Handwriting			Average.
Spelling			Good.	Craft or Needlework			Good
				Physical Ed.			Satisfactory
ARITHMETIC				**SPECIAL APTITUDES**			
Tables			Excellent.	Art			Average.
Mental			Average.	Music		Always shows	
Problems			Good.			much interest	
Mechanical			Excellent.				

PROGRESS......

Lesley always shows interest in her work which is neat and well presented. Keen and enthusiastic in class general activities she has taken the lead in Drama and Choral Verse Speaking with confidence and ability. A pleasant cooperative pupil.

M.G.Linehan.   Class Teacher

Lesley has completed a good year's work with pleasing results in both English and Arithmetic.   B.Wakefield.   Head Teacher

School re-opens on...... 9th September

Lesley's school report from Fairways Junior, 1958. (Horner collection)

Lesley's interests at this age were in dancing and in horses. From as early as the age of 2, Mum took her along to Mrs Wheeler at the Mannering School of Dancing, which seems to have been in a church hall in Westborough Road. This may have been initiated to help her overcome a tendency to shyness. The clothes and shoes needed for the tap, modern and ballet classes were mostly hand-me-downs, and as a result Lesley remembers the smell of her very first pair of new, leather ballet shoes in the 1950s. The youngsters put on shows at the Plaza in Southchurch Road. From the age of 7 or so, Lesley moved to the Georgina Miller School of Dancing.

Christmas in Westbourne Grove, 1952, with Geoffrey, Lesley and the treasured slippers. (Horner collection)

Lesley Horner's dad made her winning costume – a doll in a box – for the children's fancy-dress competition at the 1951 carnival. (Horner collection: original photo Douglas West, Whitstable)

Lesley (on her mum's lap), with Geoffrey, Auntie Edith and Stevie on Southend Pier, 1952. (Horner collection)

Lesley (right) at Mrs Wheeler's dancing school, c. 1952. (Horner collection)

As to her love of horses, she was lucky enough to be able to walk to school along the Fairways, past fields with horses in them. By the age of 8 she was a regular at the local stables. In return for mucking out, she was given a free bareback ride. Sometimes these sessions would run late into the evening, and she knew she was in trouble when she saw the glow of her dad's cigarette approaching through the woods. She'd overdone it – it could be as late as 11 p.m. – and he was coming to take her home.

Childhood games often invoked a love of horses, because then imagination could come into play – substitutes would be a bike or a pogo stick. In addition there was roller skating, the hula hoop, the skipping rope and a scooter, all enjoyed safely in their secluded close. At school, Lesley played shinty, which she describes as being like hockey with a thin stick.

At around the age of 11, Lesley felt she had to choose between horses and dance, and dance won. Lessons were now a bit more upmarket, taking place at the

SOUTHEND-ON-SEA CORPORATION

in association with

JAY-JAY PRODUCTIONS

proudly present their 1962 Pantomime Season :

"ROBINSON CRUSOE"

(version by Jerry Jerome)

Cast in order of appearance :

Danny	DONALD MACLEAN
Paddy	PATRIC KELLY
Captain and Mate	CLEAVER AND CLAMP
Will Atkins	BERT LENA
Polly Perkins	MARGARET McKECHNIE
Billy Crusoe	MARTY SWIFT
Robinson Crusoe	ROBERTA PETT
Mrs. Crusoe	JERRY JEROME
Davy Jones	DON RIVERS
Fairy Stella Maris	ANN HAVEN
Man Friday	PHIL KAUFFMAN
Citizens, Sailors etc., etc.	GEORGINA MILLER BABES and the TEN LOVELY PETS

ORCHESTRA under the direction of CECIL BARKER

MEET YOUR FRIENDS
in the newly constructed
THEATRE LICENSED BAR & COFFEE LOUNGE
Chimes sound three minutes before the curtain rises

SYNOPSIS OF SCENES

ACT ONE

Scene 1	The Docks
Scene 2	Passing Gibraltar
Scene 3	Between Decks
Scene 4	Fore Deck of the Saucy Sal
Scene 5	Main Deck
Scene 6	In the Sea
Scene 7	Davy Jones Locker

INTERVAL

ACT TWO

Scene 8	Wallamaloo Island
Scene 9	Crusoe's Hut
Scene 10	The Temple of Jewels
Scene 11	The Custom House
Scene 12	Mrs. Crusoe's Residence
Scene 13	A Hallway in the Palace
Scene 14	The Palace

PRODUCED BY JERRY JEROME

CHOREOGRAPHY BY ROBERTA PETT

Scenery specially designed and painted by JEAN BIRKUMSHAW

Costumes by ROSE OF LONDON and STAR COSTUMES

Wardrobe Supervisor .... " BILLIE " NUNN

Stage Manager (for JAY-JAY Productions) ...... DICK SMALE

Programme for Robinson Crusoe *at the Palace Theatre, 1962, featuring the Georgina Miller Babes and Don MacLean.* (Horner collection)

Arlington Rooms, opposite Chalkwell Schools, and the girls appeared regularly in local shows and took part in local competitions, including the annual Leigh Community competition. Lesley particularly enjoyed appearing on the old bandstage at carnival time, and in the pantomimes at the Palace Theatre in 1960 (*Cinderella*), 1961 (*Mother Goose*) and 1962 (*Robinson Crusoe*). The pantomimes were usually produced by Jerry Jerome, who always played the dame, and choreographed by his wife, Roberta Pett.

For Lesley, the most memorable panto was *Robinson Crusoe*, mainly because Don MacLean, he of the powerful voice, was one of the principals. (He is better known as a presenter of Radio 2's *Good Morning Sunday.*) She admits to being more than a little star-struck, and was overjoyed when he regularly saw her and one of the older dancers to the bus stop after the show. He even visited the family for tea one day, giving Lesley the opportunity to record his singing and his conversation on Dad's bulky Grundig tape-recorder – but her brother subsequently erased the tape. Whoops. She was broken-hearted when Don moved on.

These pantos were well attended, and at the end of the run, the Georgina Miller Babes reprised the panto themselves for the staff and players. Although Lesley could not sing, she played the lead in this revamp, speaking the words of the songs. This entertainment was followed by a party for the adults. So good fun was had by all.

The girls from Georgina Miller's school worked hard, as did everyone else, rehearsing on Christmas Eve, and starting the run on Boxing Day. Still, they were paid for their contribution, and Lesley made good use of her wages. She bought her first watch, and her first grown-up(ish) pleated skirt with dinky high-heeled shoes in Martin Ford in Southend.

Dancing did not stop when Lesley got home. In fact, she ruined the Marley tiles in the kitchen, and her parents had to provide a piece of plywood for her to dance on instead.

However, at 15 she was diagnosed with a slight heart murmur, and this, combined with what she felt was the need to concentrate on school work, brought an end to her dancing. School from 1958 was Westcliff High. Miss Raeburn, the Scottish head, was very strict, and insisted that all the girls had plastic square rain hats (which she pronounced 'plarstic') to add to their navy skirts, pale-blue shirts, ties and berets. There were also scratchy serge hockey skirts to contend with. Another of Lesley's pet hates was needlework, retrospectively difficult because she was left-handed.

More happily, strawberry custard was Lesley's favourite pud in the canteen at dinner time, and she enjoyed cookery, maths, science and sports. There was an outside swimming pool at the school, athletics and tennis in summer, and hockey. As hockey captain when in the lower sixth, Lesley travelled with the team to other schools at the weekend for matches, and played at the Easter Hockey Festival, where the final was usually between Southend and Westcliff High schools. As a postscript, it is fascinating to note that Lesley still uses the recipe from Westcliff High every year for her Christmas cake.

The nearest Lesley got to being in trouble during her schooldays was when she apparently broke the rule that you did not mix with boys from neighbouring schools even outside school premises. She was reprimanded for this, but did not confess until the very last minute that the boy in question was her brother, Geoffrey.

In 1962, when she was only 15, Lesley's brother was instrumental in introducing her to her future husband, Ray. Ray had been feeling ill, and, as a reward for Geoffrey's help, he brought him home in his butcher's van – the Horners had a butcher's in Rochford. This was after a lads' Friday night out at the Peter Boat and the Crooked Billet in Old Leigh followed by a trip on the big wheel at the Chalkwell Park fête – so Ray's temporary illness was probably not that unexpected.

Lesley met up with Ray again at the National Athletics in Chelmsford, where she cheered him on from the sidelines, and persuaded Geoffrey to invite him to his 18th birthday party. Their parents went away for the weekend, so that all the furniture could be moved out, leaving plenty of room for dancing to the Beatles' records, which were bought in the main from Gilbert's in London Road (the owner was a friend of her dad). As a concession to the more macho interests of

Horner's butcher's, Rochford, early 1960s. Note the Christmas turkey display. (Horner collection)

many of the boys, a back bedroom was also turned into a darts room. Even so, the noise levels were still sufficiently over the top to attract a visit from the local police, but that was all it took to bring the volume down.

Before leaving school, Lesley earned money with a paper round, and with waitressing – which included Sunday morning breakfasts – in the cafés under the arches at Westcliff and at a hotel in the same area. Most of her money went on clothes, as Dad was very keen on music and was the one who bought the records and tapes for the household.

Ray left school a few years before Lesley and went to teacher-training college for a year, but soon returned to the family trade. Lesley became head girl at Westcliff High in 1965, voted for by the pupils – not, she feels, because she was an academic, but because she was on the bossy side. The vote was considered so important that the family came home early from their first holiday abroad to find out the result (holidays since 1962 had been spent in a VW caravanette, which Dad bought with money inherited from his aunt in that year). The only downside with this role was that she could not continue as hockey captain, which was a bit of a disappointment for her.

Lesley left school with A levels in pure and applied maths. She had been considering studying sociology at Swansea University, but decided to work for the Central Electricity Generating Board in IT until she married at the age of 20 in 1968. As a couple, she and Ray favoured the cinema or eating out to more social venues, which were primarily about meeting the opposite sex. They did frequent the Grosvenor Grill in London Road, however, a coffee bar opposite Chalkwell Park.

They also attempted to learn ballroom dancing at Mimi Green's in the London Road, but Ray found only a modicum of success with the cha-cha and the twist. His lack of prowess was probably not helped by his tendency to disappear to the gents' room every time he was asked to dance with anyone but Lesley, as a result of the shortage of male partners. Friday night out with the lads, however, was sacrosanct.

On one occasion, they enjoyed taking part with friends in the Rochford Tennis Club Car Rally – in the butcher's van. Unfortunately, their friends, who sat in the back with dead rabbits hanging up around them, were not so keen.

Lesley and Ray's wedding was at St Andrew's, Rochford, on Easter Monday so that the butcher's would not have to be closed for the occasion. The reception was at Belfairs Masonic Hall, some of which – including a lively conga – was recorded by her dad and his friend. The cake was made by her brother-in-law, a baker (from the Grout family). The empire-line dress was home-made, though Lesley had to go to evening classes to improve her skills in this direction. The honeymoon in Tenerife was paid for by her new husband and was Lesley's first trip in an aeroplane.

Married life started in a two-bed detached bungalow in Rochford, which set them back £5,300, with a mortgage of £25 8s 4d per month helped by a top-up from Ray's parents. Amazingly, the couple are still there, although the bungalow has seen many changes over the years.

Until 1969, Lesley continued to commute to the CEGB, but then worked in the Horner's butcher's shop until her first daughter, Lorraine, was born in 1970. This was a period when butchers had still not been hit by excessive regulations and by supermarkets; and the business was a very successful one.

FRANCES WILLETTS

Young and Innocent

One of many Londoners living in Southend, Frances moved here with her parents and brother in 1960 from Forest Gate. She had been ill as a child, in the 1950s, and the family often spent Sundays in Thorpe Bay, utilising the beach trays – with proper cups and saucers – from the café near the Halfway House. This seems to have convinced them that it would be a good place to live and would be particularly beneficial for Frances's bronchial condition. It seems to have done the trick, at least for Frances, although ironically her mum developed rhinitis, a form of all-year-round hay fever.

Frances Willetts and Roderick on Southend beach, 1953. (Willetts collection)

It took Frances a long time to settle in her new school, Dowsett High. In London all the other 12-year-olds were wearing bras and stockings or tights, but in Southend the other girls still seemed to be wearing socks to accompany their grey uniforms, and this seems to have alienated her. Roderick, her brother, fared rather better at Southchurch Hall School for Boys, although the headmaster told him at his interview that the fashionable winkle-pickers he was wearing would not be allowed.

The family settled in a big Victorian house in Ambleside Drive, which cost her bricklayer father £1,850. Everyone got involved in doing up the house, which may well have been used by the Army during the war, but at least it sported their first bathroom. There were steam trains at the bottom of the garden, which meant that Mum's white washing did not stay white for too long. The children used to stand and watch the trains, looking out for their father returning from work. When they saw him wave from the train, they could tell Mum that he would soon be home for tea, as Southend East station was only a five-minute walk away.

At weekends and in the summer, Frances worked part-time wherever possible while at school. One job was as a washer-upper in a café in Leigh Old Town, but as they had never had washing-up liquid at home, she made the mistake of pouring a bowl of what she'd dismissed as 'strange-looking' soapy water down the sink, so she was moved on to serving ice-cream. This was not served from a machine but was dug out of a big churn. It was difficult enough scooping up the near-frozen ice-cream, but even more difficult trying to balance it on the cornet without breaking the flimsy cone structure. Practice made perfect eventually, and Frances's party-piece was filling seven cornets in one hand at the same time! She does recall skiving off one Wednesday during carnival week to enjoy time with her girlfriends, dressed up as St Trinian's schoolgirls.

Rod's part-time jobs while at school included selling ice-cream at Thorpe Bay from a cart on the beach. A white van would drop him and the cart off, and he walked up and down from Lifstan Way to Thorpe Bay Yacht Club selling ices and drinks. The van would reappear every so often to top him up. Mum, too, earned money doing odd jobs in beach cafés or in shops such as the Beach Road Bakery, which is still there.

When she was a youngster, spare time and spare money were spent in the amusement arcades and at Rossi's when it was near Southend Central station. A favourite drink at Rossi's was cold milk with ice-cream in it, a forerunner of the milkshake. When money was scarce, a popular place to meet friends and chat was at Dixons (now W.H. Smith) in the High Street.

Frances left school at 15 and began her working life as a junior typist in a modern solicitors' office in Victoria Avenue. She had been taught to type by a lady in Woodgrange Drive who charged for 'lessons', which seemed only to involve sitting girls in front of a typewriter and handing over an instruction manual. While at school, she had not received any commercial training, so she had no idea what to expect of office life; the Dictaphone machine was problematic, and as for the correspondence . . . The solicitors specialised in litigation (divorce), so the things that Frances was reading and typing about were real eye-openers to a 15-year-old. At the time, divorce seemed to be a more spiteful process, and the correspondence certainly reflected this.

Of the £3 per week that Frances then earned, at least £1 went to her mum. Her luncheon vouchers – 3s per day – meant that she had a choice of the rolls available at the café in the Talza Arcade. After six months, she and her employers parted company, and Frances rather liked the idea of getting away from the big unwieldy documents she had been required to type, with their messy, unforgiving carbon copies, but she ended up in another solicitors' in Alexandra Street. One boss's response to the excessive carbon smudges on a letter he was due to sign was to draw round them with a pen while asking 'Do you think you are working in a coal mine?' She managed to escape eventually and by the mid-1960s was commuting to London.

Frances's first regular nights out involved getting on a bus – alone – to the Odeon in Southend High Street on Fridays. Above the cinema was Victor

Frances's first marriage, at York Road Methodist Church, March 1968. (Willetts collection)

Sylvester's dance studio, where you could learn ballroom dancing, and meet boys. At the time the girls wore stiletto heels and net underskirts, and the system was such that each girl had a chance to dance with each of the men there. Saturday was a no-no, as this was couples' night. After Victor Sylvester, Frances progressed to coffee bars and the Halfway House, which held dances on a Saturday. Her first experience of a 'proper' dance was very different from ballroom dancing. For a start, it seemed that all the boys needed a good drink just to get on the dance floor, but oh, the joy of being asked for a dance.

Shades coffee bar on Southend seafront was her haunt, along with all the other local mods of the 1960s. The place was particularly packed if the Paramounts were playing in the basement. Shades sported a small dance floor with alcoves around it, and it was just the place to show off your latest mod gear. Frances remembers particularly her home-made ankle-length skirts, and her Bri-Nylon navy-blue mac that billowed as you moved. She also borrowed £5 from her dad to buy a green suede jacket, which became her pride and joy.

Specific memories are of seeing the Beatles at the Odeon in 1963 – at their first visit in May, where there was still mass hysteria but not as bad as at their October concert. Frances also saw Tony Blackburn at the Cliffs Pavilion, at the time when Radio Caroline and other pirate ships were making celebrities of disc jockeys. Tony Blackburn seems to have taken a liking to Frances's very pretty friend, Carole, and he met the girls in the bar after the show and offered them both a lift home. Unfortunately for Frances he had a tiny bright-red sports car, so she was the one in the back. And to make the evening even worse, when he pulled up outside her house, who should be standing by the front gate but her worried mum. She could not get in the door quickly enough.

As the mods graduated from coffee bars towards the end of the 1960s, the Peter Boat at Leigh became the 'in' place to go and indulge in your favourite tipple, usually cider, or vodka and lime. The pub was also popular with hippies. Rod, eighteen months older, favoured the Elms in London Road, especially after watching Southend United play football on a Saturday, because the team would turn up there for a drink afterwards. He also drank at EKCO's club in Prittlewell.

In 1968, Frances married her first husband. The wedding was a traditional white, church wedding in central Southend, with a hall for the reception. They left the celebrations early, still hungry, and had a Chinese meal in Alexandra Street, then stayed overnight at the Westcliff Hotel before a honeymoon in Cliftonville. This was the first time Frances had been in a hotel, or even away from home. She recalls the luxury of an en suite, but was a bit disappointed that they had to decorate their Morris Minor themselves as none of their friends or family had thought of doing it.

THE SCOTT SISTERS

Oh, They Do Like to Be beside the Seaside

Carol was born on the cusp of the 1950s and brought up in a council house in Ruskin Avenue with her sister Elizabeth (eight years older, and born in the Midlands) and three other siblings. Their dad, Len, born in Southend, was the chief stoker at Southend's seafront gasworks, and he and his co-workers had to work hard to keep their skin free of the black grime that went with the job. Their Uncle Jack earned his living rather differently – he worked on the Pier as a deckchair attendant, and charged trippers for a game of bow-and-arrows.

To supplement Len's income – and his interest in gambling on the greyhounds and the horses – he also held down additional part-time jobs. One of these was at Bettell's, the greengrocer's in Talza Arcade, and another was at the Kursaal, where he looked after a sideshow called The House of Many Windows. These windows were made of coloured cellophane which customers threw balls at to try and secure prizes. According to Elizabeth (always known as Blue), it was not unusual for stallholders to supplement their income by 'accidentally' dropping some of the takings into their trouser turn-ups.

Early schooldays for the Scott children were spent at Bournemouth Park School. Carol has particular recall of her very first day, when one of her early lessons was held in a small stand-alone structure in the centre of the playground, with an open fire. The head teacher, Mr Hardy, used to have a motorbike and sidecar and even wore leathers. Nearly

Left to right: Michael Scott, Carol Scott on horse, Elizabeth, Dad Len, Vicky, under the old Pier bridge, c. 1952. (Scott collection)

Carol and Mr Hardy, ex-head of Bournemouth Park School, 'reunited' in Bourton-on-the-Water, 2000. (Scott collection)

half a century later, she bumped into him when on holiday at Bourton-on-the-Water and he actually remembered her.

Twice a week, Carol had religious instruction lessons at what was called the Tin Shed alongside St Luke's Church. One of the attractions of these particular lessons was the location – next door to a tuckshop with sweets available at a farthing each. Another memory of infant school was of being the monitor responsible for making holes for straws in the tops of the bottles of tepid school milk, using a metal stick for the purpose. The uniform was a green and white check dress in the summer and a blue gymslip with white shirt in the winter.

Outside school in the 1950s, the girls recall outdoor games at a street party for the coronation in 1953, with tables along Tennyson Avenue, although the rain meant they ended up cramming themselves into the home of the obliging Mrs Haslem, a local resident. The Scotts had the first television set in Ruskin Avenue, with a 9in screen, and all and sundry were welcomed to watch the ceremony. Carol also remembers playing on the bombed-out site that later became the Co-op in Sutton Road, and 'brooking' in Priory Park (jumping in and out of the water). Then there was the pleasure of standing on the corner of Bournemouth Park Road collecting car numbers at a time when you had to wait twenty minutes for a car to pass. School holidays were often spent on the beach, taking sandwiches and 6*d* to spend on ice-cream or at Peter Pan's playground. Childhood games included hopscotch, cycling, roller skating, skipping ropes and jacks, often played in the empty roads.

One of the highlights of Carol's year was the annual carnival's final evening torchlight procession, with the colourful illuminations, especially those that lit up Never Never Land on the seafront. Their mum insisted the children had a nap before their late-night trip to see the lights, and Carol herself took part once on a float as a Chinese girl. There was also an annual Paper Boys' Christmas Party at Garons at Victoria Circus, paid for it seems by a grateful man (a paper-seller perhaps?) who had been cleared of some unmentionable offence. Then there was the annual party for the staff of the gasworks, usually at the Hope Hotel on the seafront, which included such entertainment as clowns and Punch and Judy. The local tenants' association organised coach trips a little further afield, to places

Carol in front row on left, Vicky in back row on right, Elizabeth (Blue) on right one row from back, next to Michael; coronation street party, 1952. (Scott collection)

such as Maldon; and Len would take the children once a year to London, where they visited 'anything that was free' according to Blue, walking till they dropped, and picnicking in Hyde Park. Len also treated them occasionally to a knickerbocker glory in the tea room at the Co-op, then near Victoria Circus, followed by a visit to the Kursaal funfair.

The date of 5 November for Carol and her brothers and sisters was 'A penny for the guy?' time at the greyhound stadium, then in Sutton Road. If someone had a good win, they would be extra generous to the children, and the winnings were shared out by older sister Vicky. The children were spoilt for choice as to what they spent their share on – there was the stadium fish shop where you could buy chips in newspaper for about 4*d*, two pickled onions for 1*d* and ask for crackling if you were lucky. Or there was the off-licence on the corner of Ruskin Avenue where you could buy a bottle of Tizer and a Bath biscuit or perhaps a packet of Smith's crisps with the salt in blue waxed paper. You could also boost your spending power by returning old bottles to the off-licence in exchange for 1*d*.

Carol's best friend at the time was Susan Copping, whose parents owned Fossetts Farm, quite a large agricultural spread where Waitrose is now. Their cottage was near to the crematorium. Sometimes it was Susan who accompanied

Carol on left behind the empty chair, with Vicky on her left. Paperboys' party, c. 1954. (Scott collection)

Carol to Saturday morning pictures at the Ritz, where the back of the Royals is now. This cost 6*d* downstairs, or 9*d* upstairs, with an Orange Maid drink-on-a-stick the only ice-cream option available at 3*d*. If you had a uniform – Brownies, Cubs, whatever – this was one place where you could show it off. The film show at the Ritz was preceded by a blind man playing an accordion, his guide dog bringing around the collecting box. After the cinema, it was just a few yards to the arcades on the seafront to spend a few pennies, or a visit to Peter Pan's playground.

At home, the number of tradesmen that called round in the 1950s was prolific. There was the baker with his wicker basket, the milkman with his horse and cart (progressing to an electric milk float in the 1960s), the coalman, the fish man on Sundays with primarily cockles and winkles, the Corona drinks man (Carol recalls bottles with corks), the ice-cream man, who would take your empty bowl on Sundays to fill up with vanilla (with optional sprinkles). Plus weekly visits from the Provident Cheque man (a form of loan you could use in certain shops), the dustbin men who carried the old metal dustbins on their shoulders, and the insurance man. When the gas-meter man came to read the meter, which would have been full of cash, he would always refund some of the money, and this was regarded by the Scott family almost as a financial treat.

Less of a treat were visits to the Children's Clinic, which was then in Sutton Road. This was the place where Mum acquired the necessary malt, cod liver oil, orange juice and syrup of figs (the latter for the Friday-night dose).

Queuing up for days outside Keddies in the High Street was quite an annual event when their sale was on. There was even a brass band to keep you entertained while you queued. This was a big occasion, with people taking flasks, and able to reserve in advance what they wanted to buy so that they were not gazumped when they finally got in through the entrance doors.

Carol also remembers the smell of coffee from Planters at Victoria Circus, the fountain in the entrance to R.E. Jones the jeweller, knickerbocker glories for about 2s 6d at Tomassi's (where the Royals shopping mall is now), and people dressing up to the nines to go to the Palace Theatre. Then there was the glassmaker in the window of the shop on Pier Hill who made small glass animals, in spite of the small faces pressed up against the glass for hours on end. At the bottom of the hill, the sausage shop was memorable not just for its food, but also for the giant sausage in the window with a pinny on! And further along Marine Parade, outside the Foresters Arms, was the water-melon stall, the fresh fish on sale from the fishing boats, and the rather splendid sit-on weighing machine.

To return to education, the senior school for both sisters was Wentworth. They both remember the head, Miss Marsden, as a strict figure with tweeds and brogues. At this school, boys and girls were separated by a central hall. Carol regards her time here with some nostalgia, and a fondness for its innocence. Blue has less fond memories of school days. She seems to have – with some minor regrets, perhaps – avoided doing as much work as possible, and was especially good at dodging sports activities organised by Mrs Hare, both in school and on the Jones's Memorial Ground. Blue seems to have spent a lot of time standing in the school corridor as a form of punishment, although she did like history and domestic science. The latter, incidentally, involved learning how to sterilise hairbrushes and combs, how to iron, and how to make tea 'properly', as well as cookery. After their last domestic science class, the girls had to prepare a three-course meal for the teachers, and this appeared to be a success.

Most memorably, music teacher Mrs Bonnet, complete with pince-nez, had an innovative way of loosening the children's jaws before they started singing. She got them to chew American wine gums. But this was now the swinging sixties and Carol was a teenager, so she had rather different musical tastes. When the Beatles were booked to appear at the Odeon in Southend High Street in 1963, she queued all night for tickets with sister Vicky and a friend, and then found out that their dad had won tickets in a competition set by the *Southend Standard*. They had seats upstairs in the front row but could not hear a single song because of the screaming – in which pursuit they also took part; in fact Carol lost her voice. The Odeon was always quite an experience for Carol, memorable because of its plush, red carpet, so different from the cold linoleum at home.

As a mod in the 1960s, Carol used Biba's mail-order catalogue, but also shopped for the 'right' clothes at Nats in the Talza Arcade, and at Martin and Ford's opposite the Odeon, where her young sister-in-law worked. She frequented the many coffee bars then in Southend, including Shades on the

Talza Arcade, with the Flying Dragon Chinese restaurant in the centre, early 1960s. Note the building work pre-empting the demise of this whole area. (Nicholls collection)

seafront, and remembers one dramatic bank holiday mod gathering that prevented an ambulance getting to a very ill man who subsequently died, perhaps as a result of this delay. The first disco was the Penny Farthing in Elmer Approach, which was open until 2 a.m. The Estuary Room also progressed during the 1960s from bands to groups. Another favourite venue was the Kursaal, and Carol especially liked the Wall of Death, the coconut shies and what she refers to as the tunnel of love.

To earn extra money at weekends and during school holidays, Carol worked for the Ocean Fish Restaurant (now the Wimpy) on the seafront, pouring teas and helping out for £1 per day. This helped pay for her mod haircuts and false eyelashes. An occasional flutter on bingo at the Talza Arcade could result in a meal at the newly opened Chinese restaurant nearby, the Flying Dragon. By now her two older brothers were apprenticed to the Gas Board, thanks to Dad, and sister Vicky worked for a while at E.K. Cole and as a waitress on the seafront.

Blue's memories of the 1950s and 1960s differ to some extent from Carol's as a result of the age difference, eight years being a big gap when you are young. In the 1950s, she went jiving at the Long Bar in the Palace Hotel or the Druids Hall in Chase Road, a popular venue, featuring records by Bill Haley and Elvis Presley. This was a good place to meet boys, who could then accompany her to the Kursaal on Saturday nights when they had the big bands such as Billy Cotton, Joe Loss, Johnny Dankworth and Ted Heath. Her clothes featured net underskirts, stockings with seams and diamanté ankle trims, and stilettos – and the boys all seemed to sport kiss curls.

As to the cinema, for Blue, Garons was the favourite, not just because it was the cheapest but because it seemed to specialise in rerunning old films such as Mario Lanza's, which she rather liked. The Odeon was impressive for her because of the size of the organ that played in the interval and the fountains that featured at the sides of the screen. Her favourite pubs were apparently the Victoria with its splendid fireplaces (at Victoria Circus) and the Middleton Hotel in the High Street near the railway bridge.

To pay for her social life, Blue worked as a waitress in the York Restaurant in York Road (now Iceland) from the age of 13. When she left school at 15 she found employment in Jack's shirt factory off North Avenue for a year – first ironing collars and then machining. Then her oldest brother, David, suggested a job at the newly opened Diamond Bar, which was part of Woolworths, being accessed from Alexandra Street. This horseshoe-shaped eating venue was probably the first in the town to serve hamburgers, and became a very popular meeting place. The whole area was stainless steel, and the cleaning at the end of the day was the hardest part of the job for Blue and the other staff. She started as a waitress, and then took over the cooking, which took place – innovatively – in full view of the customers. The staff wore a uniform of pinafore and little hat.

Among the regulars at the Diamond Bar were the staff of the nearby SMAC's, who specialised in car hire rather than car sales in those days. This is how Blue met John, an ex-Army lad from Shoeburyness, whose home still had gas lighting, to Blue's fascination. He invited her to the pictures, and three years later there were wedding bells at St Luke's Church in Bournemouth Park Road. Sisters Carol and Vicky were bridesmaids, and the reception was in the church hall. Their first home was at 13 Wilson Road, a one-bedroom rented flat with a shared bathroom, and this is where it was planned that their son Paul would be born in 1962. However, because Paul turned out to be a breech birth, the delivery was finally carried out at Rochford Hospital, although Blue's other three children – all born by 1970 – were delivered at home.

The young family moved to a bigger flat in Rylands Road when Paul was born, and Blue remembers lugging the heavyweight pram up the stairs every night. This pram had been paid for by Dad because he knew the owner of the shop at Victoria Circus and because he could pay off the cost in instalments. Their first house in 1967 was a council property at Mendip Crescent by Kent Elms Corner in Westcliff, which felt a bit out in the sticks to Blue, although it is of course now very built up. From Mendip, Blue's family would walk as far as Chalkwell Beach in the summer, and they were regulars at Priory Park. The children went to school at Blenheim Infants and Juniors in the 1960s.

And at the end of that decade, Carol remembers a visit to the Family Planning Clinic in Baxter Avenue at a time when you had to prove you were married or engaged before you could get appropriate advice.

PAT PARKINS

Pop and Disco

Pat and her family moved from Dagenham to King's Caravan Park on Canvey Island in 1956. She was 4 and her brother three years older. There were quite a number of moves within the space of a few years – to York Road, Southend; Valkyrie Road, Westcliff; Clifftown Road, Southend, and a flat over one of the seafront pubs in Southend. They then settled rather longer at Fairlawn Gardens, Southend.

By now, her mum was working for E.K. Cole on their production line, and her dad was a toolmaker for the Brightwell Box Company. Dad – Thomas Patrick Hamilton Irving Costello – became a bit of a local celebrity in the 1950s and early 1960s. When he had finished his day job, he found time not only for horse racing and dog racing (live at Southend and Romford), but also to establish himself as a well-known singer and compère in the bars and clubs in and around Southend.

At the end of the 1950s, Pat remembers hiding behind the organ of the Long Bar, which formed the lower part of the Palace Hotel. When her dad was appearing, she was able to sneak in before the bar officially opened, and stay there until she was discovered, as she invariably was. He was a regular at the Palace, the Esplanade pub and the Minerva pub, among others, although Pat could not sneak her way into these venues. All the pubs had a piano, or perhaps an organ, occasionally even a drummer, to accompany Tommy's singing, his style being Matt Monro-ish. But he does not seem to have been paid – except perhaps by the Palace – other than in beer.

Singing and entertaining took up most of her dad's evenings, although Mum did not always approve, especially if he brought back a bunch of the lads after a drinking session and expected them to be fed. Fried bacon and eggs at 2 a.m. was perhaps pushing his luck. Occasionally,

Pat Parkins on the beach near Peter Pan's playground, 1956. (Parkins collection)

Telephone :
SOUTHEND 63709

Mr. **RAYMOND MADDOCKS**
Resident General Manager
Mr. **HARRY THREADGOLD**
Asst. Manager
(Ex. Sunderland & Southend F. C)

THE PALACE BARS
(A BEN TRUMAN HOUSE)

PIER HILL, SOUTHEND-ON-SEA

PIER BAR   WITH   VICTORY BAR

ARTHUR HARTLEY
at the fabulous
Hammond organ

Starring

TOMMY COSTELLO
A great s'ng'ng
compere

AND

Starring both
TERRY WILLIAMS
Southends best
entertainer
&
RON REYNOLDS
London's
Frank Ifield

"Get on the trail of the hoppiest ale" or "track down a Trubrown"

Palace bars flyer, early 1960s. (Smeeton collection)

Tommy Costello, in centre with bow tie, and staff of the Palace Hotel, including Terry Williams, the blonde female impersonator, in the back row, mid-1960s. (Parkins collection: original photo Norman Davis, Westcliff)

though, Mum did go and watch Tommy singing, and must have been proud of his popularity. She got to know other entertainers in the town at the time, including Luigi, a singer with a powerful voice, and Terry Williams, a female impersonator.

Pat's first school was the Sacred Heart in Southchurch Road, the same junior school her brother attended. This was attached – literally – to the Sacred Heart Church, with old brick-built toilets in a separate block from the main schoolhouse. The priest and the headmaster had an equal say, it seems, in the running of the school. Every day included religious instruction lessons, with

Pat and brother Thomas at her first Communion, the
Sacred Heart, Southchurch, 1957. (Parkins collection)

special emphasis on the catechism, and Communion, Confirmation and Confession preparation before the age of 11. On Sundays, the family attended the same church, although their last move meant they transferred to the congregation of the St John Fisher Church at Prittlewell (Cuckoo Corner).

In her spare time, Pat was happy to play street games with a skipping rope or ball, go bait digging and fishing from the jetty near to the Pier, or watch football with her mum, dad (if he was not working in one capacity or another) and brother, another Thomas. Thomas junior played for the Southend United boys' team, winning medals for his efforts. Dad's carpentry skills were evidenced at one particular birthday when he presented Pat with a handmade dolls' house – which she still possesses. Another birthday treat was a visit to Southend's first Chinese restaurant, the Flying Dragon near Victoria Circus, which replaced the New Vic cinema.

Particular childhood memories are of the annual carnivals, especially the torchlight procession on Saturday evenings, and the annual choosing of the carnival queen at the Odeon, which followed the featured film. Pat remembers ballroom-dancing lessons at the Victor Sylvester Dance Studio, atop this same Odeon in Southend High Street. These took place on Saturday mornings, with a whole roomful of children (boys and girls), sometimes live music as well as records, and with someone on stage giving instructions. The revolving silver ball in the centre of the ornate setting was a particularly fascinating part of these sessions.

At weekends, Pat and her family would visit her nan in Dagenham, and this is where they usually spent Christmas. The front room with tree and presents inside would be locked, tantalisingly, until Christmas Day. Sometimes the Costellos would go up to London at the weekend on the steam train to Fenchurch Street, especially if there was a big Catholic procession in the East End, which was not unusual.

In 1962, Pat moved up to St Bernard's School in Milton Road, Westcliff. This was a very strict Catholic school, with the Angelis bell rung every hour for the nuns in the attached convent. Only a couple of the nuns were actually teachers, for science and religious education. The summer uniform here included a straw boater and white gloves and the winter uniform boasted a felt hat similar to a bowler.

Odeon, Southend, flyer, c. 1964. (Parkins collection)

The school had a grammar stream for those who had passed their eleven–plus exam, and a secondary modern stream for the rest. But everyone used the on–site chapel and the swimming pool in Valkyrie Road, which used to be a part of St Bernard's when it was a private school. This pool was closed in the early 1960s (it is now a leisure centre), and swimming then took place at the Westcliff pool on the seafront. There was a great emphasis on sport and on winning medals, but there were also lessons in deportment, speech training and ballroom dancing, apparent hangovers from the days of private schooling.

Away from school in the 1960s, Pat was spoiled for choice in Southend when it came to seeing live pop performances. Concerts at the Odeon in the High Street did not feature just one star but perhaps half a dozen, and Pat remembers seeing the Searchers, the Hollies, the Walker Brothers, the Kinks, Dusty Springfield – and the Bachelors, with her mum. Mum did go to see the Walker Brothers with

Pat and Thomas with Mum and Dad in Fairlawn Gardens, mid-1960s. Note Pat's transistor radio and Thomas's guitar – that he could not play. (Parkins collection)

Pat but was put off similar evenings by the headache-inducing screaming, not just inside the Odeon but outside at the stage door. Pat was not allowed to queue overnight for tickets for the Beatles, however, as she was too young. Apart from the Odeon, Pat also ventured a few miles further to see the Who at the Kingsway in Hadleigh, a big old theatre/cinema where Morrison's supermarket is now.

Pop music was also important at home, and the children were allowed a transistor radio each, to listen to pirate radio stations. Pat hid the radio under her pillow when she wanted to listen to Radio Luxembourg late at night, especially if the Top Twenty were being played.

Pat's husband, Bob, was more of a Rolling Stones fan than a Beatles fan and he saw them twice at the Odeon in Southend in the 1960s. He recalls that on one of these evenings, one of the security men was being thrust forward with such force by the screaming fans that he pushed over a whole row of seats at the front of the

Bob (middle row, left) and pals at the Kursaal, early 1960s. (Parkins collection)

stalls. Even the Stones themselves got involved in removing some of those girls who had ended up on the stage – by the simple expedient of throwing them over one shoulder and dumping them in the side aisles. Bob also recalls a lesser-known coffee bar from the period – the Three Monkeys in Southchurch Avenue.

Southend's Golden Jubilee year was celebrated in 1964, and for Pat and Bob, who didn't know each other then, the main attraction of these celebrations was the 1*d* special price for all the rides at the Kursaal. Pat had at least four rides on her favourite, the water chute, competing with local schoolchildren who had been given the day off.

In 1966, Tommy Costello died tragically in an accident at Brightwell's at the age of just 40. Pat was 14, and did not go to the funeral, but stayed at home to organise the food. She remembers him as a man who worked hard and played hard. Not long after, the family moved to a bungalow at Eastwood, Leigh-on-Sea.

Pat now embarked on a two-year secretarial course at St Bernard's, having secured one of the limited places available for this particular option. After achieving the requisite RSA and Pitman's passes, she found a job with P&O in London as a shorthand-typist in the Fleet Personnel Division. Neither she nor any of her friends wanted to work locally – London was far more of an attraction. (Pat will always remember her first trip to Carnaby Street as a young teenager when she saw Peter and Gordon in one of the shops at the time when they were riding high in the pop charts.)

Her brother, however, did work locally, for a printing company. Any hopes he had had earlier of professional football were foiled by a road accident when Thomas was just 15: he was knocked down by a car at Cuckoo Corner, sustaining serious injuries, including a fractured skull and collarbone, causing a knock-on effect not only on his football but also on his education at St Thomas More School.

Before Bob met Pat, he was a ride attendant at the Kursaal at weekends, and an apprentice electrician during the week. One ride was similar to a tunnel of love ride, and another featured individual cars manoeuvring their way round a figure-of-eight electric track that incorporated a bridge. In the early 1970s, he was back there for a few weeks as a seasonal maintenance electrician while waiting for a job he had lined up with the electricity board.

The couple met in the late 1960s at Through till Two, one of the area's first disco/clubs, which was part of the Elms in London Road, Leigh. Friday and Saturday nights featured a DJ and there was new, trendy, fluorescent lighting. Southend's most famous nightclub, TOTS (Talk of the South), arrived later in Lucy Road, taking the place of Frank's Cash Bingo where blackjack was also featured.

By now, Pat was on the fringes of the mod circuit, although Bob was more of a rocker. She favoured mohair suits made at a York Road tailors, complete with Ben Sherman shirts. He was more your quiff and sideburns man, although these are no longer in evidence.

MARILYN
BUDGEN

Sewing and Binding

Although Marilyn was born later than the other contributors to this book, she remembers sharing the family's terraced house in Ilfracombe Road with an elderly lady who was in the Salvation Army. This spinster lived upstairs; Marilyn's dad (an upholsterer) and mum (a seamstress) lived downstairs with their young daughter. It is the Army uniform she particularly remembers. They inherited the house from its owner when she died in the 1950s.

As a young child in this decade, Marilyn enjoyed motorboat rides on the boating lake alongside the Pier, although the petrol engine was pretty smoky. The carousel further along the promenade, outside the Foresters pub, was memorable for the free sticks of Southend rock that were handed out to customers.

One thing that held Marilyn's attention for considerable periods of time was the Guinness clock, near the public toilets west of the Pier (originally at the top of the cliffs near the lift). This was one of several ostentatious Guinness clocks that disappeared in the 1960s, featuring a moving toucan, with the slogan 'Guinness is Good For You', and a whole moving parade of jungle animals every fifteen minutes, culminating in an appearance by characters from *Alice in Wonderland*, principally the Mad Hatter. It was even illuminated at night. A real joy to behold – and it was free to watch.

A favourite weekend activity was walking out on the mudflats with her dad, collecting shells and picking up crabs left behind in pooled hollows. Mum was not too keen on these being brought home, so they ended up back in the sea. When the tide was in, they picnicked on the sand – with crab sandwiches! Dad would buy lemonade from the Castle pub and take it onto the beach, and all of them swam on occasions.

When their next-door neighbours (Jack and Jill, really!) moved to Thorpe Bay, the family decided to move with them, and they ended up next door to each other once again. Jack was a builder and helped Marilyn's father with the refurbishing that was required. The garden eventually produced tomatoes, runner beans and marrows; Dad preferred raising vegetables to flowers, and even invested in a greenhouse.

By 1964 Marilyn had moved from Hamstel Road Juniors to Dowsett High School for Girls in Boston Avenue, Southend. Only the egg and spoon race on

Guinness clock, Southend cliffs, 1950s. (Dalton collection)

1967 carnival procession from the cliffs at Westcliff. (Peter Ashton collection)

sports day and the roly-poly pudding at dinner-time have stayed with Marilyn since her Hamstel Road days. At Dowsett, it seems that headmistress Miss FitzSimons measured the girls' skirts once minis had become popular – and she was not averse to doing this while the girls waited at the bus stop, to their ongoing embarrassment.

Otherwise, the nit nurse, based in the Warrior Square Clinic (where the swimming pool is now), seems to have made more of an impression on Marilyn at this age than her teachers. She does remember struggling with needlework homework at Dowsett, in particular a multicolour striped corduroy dress with a mini skirt and a long zip at the front. The only way she could finish it by the deadline was by calling on the assistance of a family friend, who was also quite handy with a needle, and who was nearer to Dowsett High than Marilyn's family.

This 'Aunt' Ivy, and 'Uncle' Bob, friends of the family, had a newsagent's and sweet shop in Park Street, Southend, and they lived over the premises. They called Marilyn 'kipper feet' as a result of her clumsiness in the shop, when she once knocked over a bottle of very smelly disinfectant. Thanks to a contact of Uncle Bob's at the *Southend Standard*'s offices in Clifftown Road, Marilyn was lucky enough to get tickets not only for the Beatles' 1963 concert at the Odeon in Southend High Street, but also for the Rolling Stones, who appeared subsequently at the same venue. On both occasions, she was accompanied by her mum.

For a while, Marilyn's mum worked part-time in a small factory in Park Street, and her dad worked for a nearby upholsterer's. There was not a lot of time for leisure activities, but there was one visit to the airport restaurant in the 1960s, a very smart venue at the time. The best feature about the restaurant for Marilyn, however, was its views of the aircraft, and she was fascinated to see the cars driving on, en route to Jersey. The Christmas treat would be the Palace Theatre pantomime, and in the summer there was Punch and Judy at the end of the Pier, viewed from blue and white striped deckchairs. After school, Marilyn used to spend time riding her Raleigh bicycle, which she named Thunderflash. Her mum also rode a bicycle, when the area was more rural and with far less traffic. After Marilyn's sister Sharon was born in 1968, Mum added a child's seat for Sharon.

This was the year Marilyn left school, and she worked for a while as a junior, mainly making teas, at a printer's in Shoeburyness. This was near to where her dad was working, and they used to meet up at lunchtimes and have sandwiches together on a convenient bench seat. When this printer's closed down a few months later, Marilyn joined Eden Fisher, another large printer's in Stock Road, Southend. Eden Fisher produced telephone directories as well as popular magazines such as *Yachts and Yachting*, the *Grocer* and even *Men Only*, which caused a few stirrings in the bindery where Marilyn worked. This was an all-female department, with dozens of women including many part-timers, all wearing nylon overalls. They spent their time glueing the spines and finishing off the publications.

Her employers had an occasional social do at the local rugby club. As a teenager at the end of the 1960s, Marilyn favoured the Elms in London Road, which featured a disco Through Till Two, but, sadly, she had to be home by midnight.

CONCLUSION

I hope you have enjoyed reading these nostalgic recollections of Southend in the 1950s and the 1960s as much as I enjoyed hearing them. Although I was living in east London then, I also have fond memories of the annual Carnival, Never Never Land, Rossi's ice-creams and the Kursaal. My family album boasts pictures of Dad with his trousers rolled up, exposing bony white feet to the sun's rays, and, yes, he wore a handkerchief on his head, knotted at each corner, to protect his bald pate.

Deliberately included are all age groups, from Harry Day, now in his eighties, to Marilyn Budgen, thirty years younger. But, in spite of the age differences, and the diverse range of backgrounds, many memories are shared. No doubt their recollections will have prompted older visitors and Southenders to say 'yes, I remember that', but hopefully will also have shown newer generations in the town that their parents and grandparents knew how to earn a crust, how to amuse themselves, and how to appreciate everything they had, however minimal that might have been. For older readers, wherever you live, these memories are bound to have struck a chord, and will no doubt share some common ground with your own memories of the period. For all readers, of all ages, there should also have been anecdotes that give an insight into elements of the town, and what went on there, that come as a complete surprise.

Fifty years on, the town still has its day trippers, but most of these are now in cars rather than trains and coaches. It is commuters who are attracted to twenty-first-century Southend, because it is near to London and yet retains the feel of a 'holiday' resort. More sand has actually been added to Southend's beaches in recent years, and luxury – always luxury – apartments have replaced many decaying sea-front hotels.

The Carnival survives, in a diminished form, and Southend now sports an annual air show, a university campus, a pedestrianised High Street, a state-of-the-art Pier entrance and lift, and a revamped Kursaal advertising itself as 'The Magic Returns'. Interestingly, the nearby Foresters pub has an even prouder sign: 'The Magic Never Went Away'. I hope that the 'magic' stays with you.